MILITARY MEMOIRS

Edited by
Brigadier Peter Young
D.S.O., M.C., M.A., F.S.A., F.R.HIST.S.

W Sherwin sculp

Richard. Atkyns. Esq. Effigies.

MILITARY MEMOIRS
The Civil War

Richard Atkyns

Edited by

BRIGADIER PETER YOUNG, D.S.O., M.C., M.A., F.S.A.,
F.R.HIST.S.

John Gwyn

Edited by

NORMAN TUCKER, F.R.HIST.S.

ARCHON BOOKS
1968

© Longmans, Green and Co Ltd 1967
First published 1967

This edition first published in the
United States of America by Archon Books, 1968,
Hamden, Connecticut

Printed in Great Britain by
W. & J. Mackay & Co Ltd, Chatham

SBN: 208 00632 X

Contents

Maps etc

General Introduction
to the Series

by PETER YOUNG

Dr Johnson: *Every man thinks meanly of himself for not having been a soldier, or not having been at sea.*
Boswell: *Lord Mansfield does not.*
Dr Johnson: *Sir, if Lord Mansfield were in a company of admirals and generals who'd seen service he'd wish to creep under the table.*

None can doubt that Samuel Johnson, so formidable with tongue and pen, was also stout of heart. Yet it would be wrong to suppose that these remarks on military service were not inspired by a genuine sentiment. One suspects that he was a bit of a fire-eater at heart. For all his wisdom he could envy the exploits of less-learned contemporaries who faced powder and shot. It is an attitude that endures even as late as the last half of the twentieth century.

It is the common lot of fighting men that they have little to show for their efforts. Their satisfaction seldom comes in the shape of material rewards, unless they are at the very top of their profession. They must be content with the private feeling that they have played their part. It may be no more complicated than the atavistic instinct to strike a blow for hearth and home, the grim satisfaction of the Gallic warrior who had killed a Roman.

But nowadays it is not given to everyone to be a soldier, or to serve in the air or on the seas. One earns no great reputation as a seer by predicting that the memoirs of those who serve in World War III will be somewhat brief, or that the struggle itself will be nasty. If people are still interested in wars, it may be better for them to satisfy their curiosity by pondering those of the past rather than provoking those of the future.

In planning a series of this sort there are a bewildering variety of factors to be considered. Of these perhaps the chief to be taken into account is the fundamental question: 'Why do people read Military History?' Is it because truth is more attractive than fiction? Baron de Marbot, although his tales had unquestionably improved in the telling, has an interest which Brigadier Gerard, despite the narrative skill of Conan Doyle, cannot rival. Marbot's memory could play him false in matters of detail, but not as to the sense of period. He brings to life the atmosphere of the Grand Army in which he served. Marbot, regrettably, is too well known, both in French and English, to parade with the veterans of this series. We have endeavoured to present memoirists who for one reason or another are relatively unknown to the English-speaking public.

In modern times memoir-writing seems to have become the prerogative of generals. One is not, however, without hopes of finding a voice or two from the ranks to conjure up the fields of Flanders or the deserts of North Africa. Of course, we have not rejected generals altogether. But on the whole we have tried to rescue 'old swordsmen' from oblivion rather than, say, a religious enthusiast, like Colonel Blackader—more concerned with the salvation of his soul than the deployment of his battalion. The fighting soldier is more attractive than an officer with a distinguished series of staff appointments to his credit; the tented field has an appeal which the dull round of garrison life cannot rival.

If such knowing officers as Captains Kincaid and Mercer or Monsieur de la Colonie, or such hard-bitten foot soldiers as Rifleman Harris or Sergeant Wheeler do not appear here, it is only because their excellent narratives are still readily obtainable.

We have avoided those veterans who, their Napier at their elbow, submerge their personal recollections in a mass of ill-digested secondhand campaign history. These are the most maddening of all. What details they could have given us had they chosen to! One reads that Colonel So-and-so dined with General Such-and-such. But why can't the fellow go on to tell us whether the general kept a good table, or what sort of conversationalist he was? Was he liked by his men? There is all the difference in the world between Rifleman Harris, who gives us such a wonderful picture of General Robert Craufurd on the retreat to Corunna, and Bragge, who fought at Salamanca and whose Journal tells us exactly nothing about it!

The trouble is that memoirists take so much for granted. They assume that we know all about the military organization and tactics of their day. And so we must just be thankful for small mercies. You will not get a fight on every page, but gradually a picture is built up. One comes to visualize the manners of a bygone age, to see how people then could endure the privations of a campaign, the rough surgery of the battlefield, or the administrative neglect of their commanders. In the end we come almost to speak their language, and to hear them speak.

When they are promoted or rewarded we can share their pleasure. *'C'était un des plus beaux jours de ma vie!'* Marbot naïvely remarks when recounting the successes of his younger days, and we are almost as pleased as he.

But if you prefer to read these adventures rather than to emulate them, that, too, is understandable.

'How sweet the music of a *distant* drum.'

Acknowledgements

We are indebted to the following for permission to reproduce copyright material: Chatto and Windus Ltd and Indiana University Press for an extract from *The Memoirs of James II*, edited by A. Lytton Sells, and the Editor of the *Journal of the Society for Army Historical Research* for an edited version of 'The Vindication of Richard Atkyns', by Brigadier Peter Young. We are grateful to Mr Bruce Stevenson, F.L.A., for compiling the Index.

Note: Spelling has been modernised, except for that of proper names. The punctuation remains unaltered. Editorial insertions appear in italics within square brackets.

Chronology

1642
23 Oct. Battle of Edgehill
12 Nov. Storming of Brentford

1643
19 Jan. Battle of Braddock Down
2 Feb. Storming of Cirencester
11 Apr. Fight at Little Dean
12 Apr. Fight at Ripple Field
16 Apr. Essex besieges Reading
23 Apr. Action at Launceston
25 Apr. Caversham Fight
27 Apr. Surrender of Reading
16 May Battle of Stratton
10 June Chewton Fight
30 June Battle of Adwalton Moor
5 July Battle of Lansdown
13 July Battle of Roundway Down
26 July Storming of Bristol
10 Aug.–5 Sept. Siege of Gloucester
2 Sept.–11 Oct. Siege of Hull
20 Sept. First Battle of Newbury

1644
29 Mar. Battle of Cheriton
29 June Battle of Cropredy Bridge
2 July Battle of Marston Moor
21 and Royalist victories near
31 Aug. Lostwithiel
2 Sept. Surrender of Essex's army
27 Oct. Second Battle of Newbury
9 Nov. Prince Rupert withdraws
the Royalist artillery from
Donnington Castle

1645
14 June Battle of Naseby
23 Sept. Surrender of Devizes to
Cromwell
c. 30 Sept. Gwyn joins the garrison of
Faringdon Castle

1646
5 May King Charles I surrenders
to the Scots at Newark
24 June Surrender of Oxford and
of Faringdon Castle

1647
30 Jan. The Scots hand over the
King to Parliament and
quit Newcastle

1648 The Second Civil War
1 June Fairfax storms Maidstone
7 July Action at Kingston. Earl
of Holland defeated
11 July Surrender of Pembroke
17–20 Aug. Battle of Preston
28 Aug. Surrender of Colchester

1649
30 Jan. London: execution of
King Charles I
The Hague: murder of
Dr Isaac Dorislaus, the
Parliament's Ambassador
Aug. Earl of Kinnoull leaves
Holland
Sept. Kinnoull reaches Kirkwall,
Orkney

1650
10 Jan. Montrose sails for Scotland
27 Apr. Colonel Strachan defeats
Montrose at Carbisdale
21 May Edinburgh: execution of
Montrose

1652 The First Dutch War
1653–4 Marquis of Glencairn's
rising in Scotland
1657 King Charles II raises six
regiments in Flanders for
the Spanish service
Gwyn commissioned as
lieutenant in the Royal
Regiment of Guards

1658
3 June Battle of Dunkirk Dunes.
Gwyn taken
3 Sept. Death of Oliver Cromwell
1660
29 May King Charles II enters
London

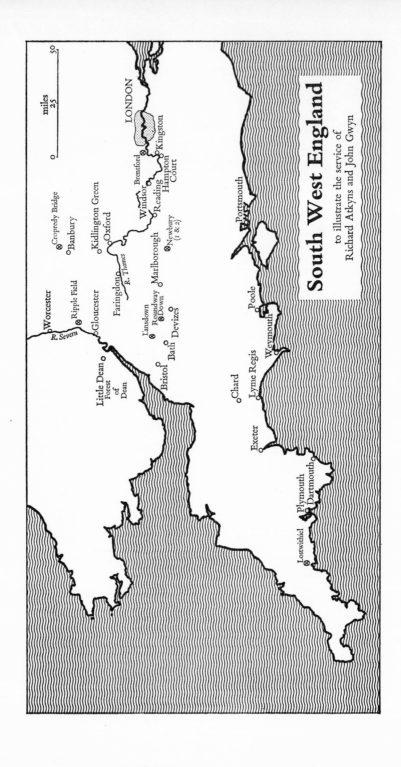

South West England

to illustrate the service of
Richard Atkyns and John Gwyn

Richard Atkyns

Introduction

Few indeed of the junior officers of either party recorded their memories of the Civil Wars. It is this that gives *The Vindication of Richard Atkyns Esquire* an importance beyond its interest as a singularly human document.

Atkyns served King Charles for less than a year, but in that time he saw much fighting, including the battles of Lansdown and Roundway Down. His account goes far to supplement the better-known narratives of Lord Hopton and Colonel Walter Slingsby.[1] *The Dictionary of National Biography* traces his career, though he figures there not for his military prowess, but for his writings on typography.

For more than a century his family had lived at Tuffley, near Gloucester; he was educated at first by two inefficient clerical tutors, later going to the Free (Crypt) School in Gloucester. At the age of fourteen he went up to Balliol College, Oxford, as a gentleman commoner, remaining in residence for two years. He could not 'read a Greek or Latin Author with pleasure', and so it does not seem likely that he took a degree. He went on to Lincoln's Inn, but 'receiving some disgust at his entrance' was soon recalled, afterwards travelling in France with a son of Lord Arundel of Wardour. After a few months abroad this youth died from getting 'a Heat and a Cold at Tennis', and so Atkyns returned home.

When he was twenty-one, in 1636, his father died, leaving him £800 a year. He writes: 'after the days of Mourning were accomplished, I put off my Hounds, put £200 in my Purse, and came to London, and kept my Coach'. As a courtier he was not a success: 'At Court I found my self guilty of three Imperfections, that would hinder my preferment there: A Blushing modesty, a Flexible disposition, and no great diligence'; failings which he again attributes to himself in later life.

Atkyns tells us little of his tastes or his personality. According to his own account he was in middle age, fat, sweaty and gouty, though Lady Atkyns was probably going too far when she accused him of being a great swearer and a drunkard. On the contrary, he was something of a puritan, highly approving of his old uncle, Baron Atkyns, who had public prayers in his house no less than four times daily. He also tells us

[1] *Bellum Civile.*

3

'I never could abide Tobacco in my life'. He mentions a visit to Mr Lawes's house, and we may suppose that he had a taste for music.

Early in 1640 Atkyns, then about twenty-five years old, married Martha, Lady Acheson, a lady of considerable fortune. Nothing of great interest befell him in the two years before the Civil War broke out, though he succeeded in impairing his fortune by lending money to an uncle named Sandys, who lived at The Vyne, in Hampshire.

The part of *The Vindication* dealing with the first Civil War is printed below. After the Restoration, Atkyns was made a deputy-lieutenant for Gloucestershire, a J.P. and a militia officer. He was also appointed to an agency for the Crown, connected with printing. He published an anonymous pamphlet entitled 'The Original and Growth of Printing', which he reprinted in 1664 under his name. His fame rests on this work, by which he hoped to prove that the right of printing belonged to the Crown alone. It has been said that Atkyns's case rested on 'a mere fable', though it has not been shown whether he invented it or was duped by others. Certainly he hoped to receive the office of patentee, and so to restore his shattered fortunes. It does not seem that he did indeed gain any material advantage from this publication, for within three years he found himself imprisoned in the Marshalsea for debt, brought there partly by his own imprudence, but still more by the extravagance of his wife, who by this time had come to hate him.

The Vindication, as the title implies, is Atkyns's *apologia pro vita sua.* His object is to present his actions, and especially those that had landed him in prison, in the best possible light. In so far as the war service of his youth is concerned, he certainly succeeds. The whereabouts of Atkyns's original MS is not now known, but there is a copy of the first edition in the British Museum, from which the extract here printed is taken. It seems certain from the Preface[1] that *The Vindication*, which appeared in 1669, was written during his imprisonment and published as soon as it was ready for the press. After the lapse of a quarter of a century Atkyns made occasional slips, omitted a week or two here and there, and evidently remembered no dates. Nevertheless he had a great memory for detail, and a good eye for country. His accounts of Lansdown and Roundway Down may be compared with those of the Parliamentarian captain, Edward Harley, in volume III of the Portland MSS, published by the Historical Manuscripts Commission.

---

[1] 'I found it necessary to bring in the most considerable Passages of my whole Life, without which, my Vindication alone would have seemed imperfect and abrupt, the Causes of it relating to more than Thirty Years since.'

Atkyns, with his rather self-conscious piety and his lack of humour, was hardly the typical Cavalier officer. Nevertheless he seems to have been a good man in action and to have won the confidence of his Colonel, Prince Maurice. He was thought sufficiently capable to be made Adjutant-General of the horse, and with reasonable good luck might have been knighted for his gallantry at Roundway Down. His narrative breathes new life into these battles of long ago. Here is a man who watched Prince Rupert storm Bristol; who saw Sir Bevil Grenvile and his pikemen save the day at Lansdown; and who drove the Colonel of the 'Lobsters' from the field of Roundway Down.

Nobody who reads his account of Chewton Fight can doubt that he had courage and dash. It is strange that he should have been so obtuse as to suppose that after Bristol the King's crown was 'settled upon his head again'. Had he not then resigned his troop, we might have had stirring accounts of the battles of Newbury and Naseby. Or, of course, some obscure musketeer might have kept him from the Marshalsea, and us from his Memoirs. . . .

The first Civil War lasted from 1642 to 1646. Captain Richard Atkyns's service was confined to the second year of the war, 1643. His regiment, Prince Maurice's Horse, belonged at first to the King's main army, but in May was sent with others to join the Western Army, which was dangerously short of cavalry.

During the early months of 1643 the Royalists, who were also short of arms, remained on the defensive around Oxford. Their offensive operations were for the most part attempts to clear their communications with their recruiting areas in North and South Wales. Atkyns was present at Rupert's first and unsuccessful attempt to take Bristol (7 March), then the second city in the Kingdom. In April he took part in the brief campaign by which Prince Maurice foiled Sir William Waller's attempt to overrun an important Royalist area, Monmouthshire and the Forest of Dean. This led to an indecisive skirmish at Little Dean, of which Atkyns gives us our fullest contemporary account, and a sharp action at Ripple Field (12 April), where Waller suffered his first serious check. There are only two known accounts of this affair, and it is unfortunate that Atkyns is content merely to record that he was there.

Meanwhile the Parliamentarian Captain-General, the Earl of Essex, had laid siege to Reading as a preliminary to an advance up the Thames Valley against the King's capital at Oxford. Atkyns took part in King Charles's abortive attempt to relieve the town, which ended in a serious repulse at Caversham Bridge (25 April). *The Vindication* gives us much detail that is otherwise quite unknown.

The rest of Atkyns's service was with the Western Army, which, after clearing Cornwall by a series of victories, by-passed Exeter and the other Parliamentarian strongholds in Devon, and advanced into Somerset, to join hands with a detachment from the 'Oxford' Army. This was an enterprising piece of strategy, and the Parliamentarian general, Sir William Waller, whose previous successes had won him the nickname of 'William the Conqueror', was hard put to it to make head against this victorious army.

After the hack-and-gallop affair at Chewton Mendip (10 June), of which Atkyns gives far the best account, the Cavaliers reached Bath, where they stormed Waller's formidable position at Lansdown (5 July). The accidental destruction, next day, of their powder, compelled them to march to Devizes. Here the tenacious Cornish infantry held out, though the town was not fortified, while the cavalry, including our author, broke out and made for Oxford.

Reinforced by two brigades of horse, they returned and routed Waller at the astonishing battle of Roundway Down (13 July), where a force consisting of some 1,800 cavalry utterly defeated a balanced force, horse, foot and guns, numbering at least 4,500. This brilliant affair led to Rupert's capture of Bristol (26 July), for Waller had drawn out much of the garrison to build up the army which he lost at Devizes.

Of Roundway Down, as of Lansdown, Richard Atkyns tells us much that is not to be found elsewhere, giving us battle pieces scarcely to be matched in the war reporting of the seventeenth century. He has a flair for detail which gives his narrative great conviction. The regiment in which he served was to win further distinction at Cheriton, Naseby and elsewhere, but its exploits are only known from snatches of information in ancient diaries and diurnals. It was never to find another chronicler to rival Captain Richard Atkyns.

In the narrative that follows the somewhat puritanical 'Sighs or Ejaculations' have been omitted. The more interesting of Atkyns's marginal notes have been used as headings in the text. His original narrative is only broken up by the 'Sighs', but here it has been thought convenient to give a section to each of the main engagements.

PETER YOUNG

The Vindication of Richard Atkyns

As no cities nor counties were free from preparations for War as their affections inclined them, so the parts about Gloucester . . . happened to be most unanimous for the Parliament, which was contrary to my judgement: for I am persuaded, that none that heard the Lord Strafford's trial, and weighed the concessions of the King in Parliament, could conscientiously be against him; but 'twas now too late to remove from thence; for fears, and jealousies, had so generally possessed the kingdom, that a man could hardly travel through any market town, but he should be asked whether he were for the King, or Parliament. In this nick of time my servant Erwing (who presently after my marriage, betook himself to the Gen d'Arms in France) hearing of the war in England came over and proferred his service to me again; whom I received as before: and being well known to his fidelity, I sent him to London to his brethren the Scots, to give me the best intelligence he could; who did it most truly, and prophetically; and as an argument of his affection to me, refused a lieutenant's place of horse on the Parliament's side, to continue my servant. Him I employed to train up my horse, and make them bold; under one Forbes his countryman, who was then governor of Gloucester; and soon after the battle of Edghill [*23 October 1642*], I waited upon the Lord Chandos to Oxon, not intending at that time, to stay any longer than to present myself to the King, and to assure him of my duty and affections: but whilst I stayed there, I received intelligence, that my being at Oxon was publicly known at Gloucester; so that I could not return in safety; but sent for the men and horses I left behind to come hither after me, and when the Lord Chandos had accepted of a commission to raise a regiment of horse, and mustered his own troop, he gave me a commission for a troop under him,[1] which I raised with such success, that within one month, I mustered 60 men besides officers, and almost all of them well armed; Master [*John*] Dutton giving me 30 steel backs, breasts and head pieces, and two men and horses completely armed: and this was done upon duty, without any

---

1 Atkyns's commission was dated 22 January 1643 (BM Harleian MS, 6852, f. 1).

advance of money, or quarters assigned; wherein every fourth or fifth man was lost.

But as some were lost, others were added; for one Powell a cornet of the Parliaments, with two troopers, (all very well horsed and armed,) came into my troop at Oxford: I carried him to the King, and begged his pardon, which the King graciously granted; and in token thereof, gave him his hand to kiss; but asked him for his commission, which when he saw; he said, he never saw any of them before; desired to keep it, and put it up in his pocket, and gave him good counsel, with very great expressions of his grace and favour to me.

My troop I paid twice out of mine own purse, and about a fortnight after, at the siege of Bristoll [7 March 1642/3],[1] I mustered 80 men besides officers;[2] whereof 20 of them gentlemen that bore arms: (here the swearing captains put the name of the Praying Captain upon me, having seen me sometimes upon my knees.) The Lord Chandos afterwards (though I had the honour to be allied to him) used my troop with that hardship, that the gentlemen unanimously desired me to go into another regiment; which his Lordship understanding, thought to affix me to his by a council of war; but failing therein, I was admitted into Prince Maurice's regiment, which was accounted the most active regiment in the army, and most commonly placed in the out quarters; which gave me more proficiency as a soldier, in half a year's time, than generally in the Low Countries in 4 or 5 years; for there did hardly one week pass in the summer half year, in which there was not a battle or skirmish fought, or beating up of quarters; which indeed lasted the whole year, insomuch as for three weeks at most, I commanded the forlorn-hope thrice.

Little Dean, 11 April 1643[3]

The first was at Little Deane, in the Forest of Deane, under the con-

---

[1] Prince Rupert attempted Bristol on 7 March 1643, but the operation can hardly be dignified with the name of a siege.

[2] The commissioned officers of a troop were the captain, lieutenant, cornet and quartermaster, but Atkyns may mean to include the three corporals and the trumpeters.

[3] Waller, advancing from Chepstow, arrived at Little Dean by six in the morning, intending to beat up Prince Maurice in his quarters. The Prince, however, withdrew without loss to a hill not far away. Waller took possession of the village, but after two hours' fighting was driven out with the loss of sixty men (Mercurius Aulicus, 15th Week).

duct of the then Lord Grandison, against Sir William Waller's army; in which was a remarkable accident: for no sooner had I received the word of command, but my charging horse fell a trembling and quaking that he could not be kept upon his legs; so that I must lose my honour by an excuse, or borrow another horse presently [*i.e. immediately*]; which with much ado I did of the Lord Chandos his gentleman of the horse, leaving twice as much as he was worth with him. The charge was seemingly as desperate as any I was ever in; it being to beat the enemy from a wall which was a strong breastwork, with a gate in the middle; possessed by above 200 musketeers, besides horse: we were to charge down a steep plain hill, of above 12 score yards in length; as good a mark as they could wish: our party consisting of between two and three hundred horse, not a man of them would follow us, so the officers, about 10 or 12 of us, agreed to gallop down in as good order as we could, and make a desperate charge upon them; the enemy seeing our resolutions, never fired at us at all, but run away; and we (like young soldiers) after them, doing execution upon them; but one Captain Hanmer being better horsed than myself, in pursuit, fell upon their ambuscade and was killed horse and man: I had only time enough to turn my horse and run for my life. This party of ours, that would not be drawn on at first, by this time, seeing our success; came into the town after us, and stopped our retreat; and finding that we were pursued by the enemy, the horse in the front, fell back upon the rear, and they were so wedged together, that they routed themselves, so as there was no passage for a long time: all this while the enemy were upon me, cutting my [*buff*] coat upon my armour in several places, and discharging pistols as they got up to me, being the outermost man; which Major Sheldon declared to my very great advantage: but when they pursued us to the town, Major Leighton had made good a stone house, and so prepared for them with musketeers; that one volley of shot made them retreat: they were so near me, that a musket bullet from one of our own men took off one of the bars of my cap I charged with, and went through my hair and did me no hurt: but this was only a forlorn party of their army to face us, whilse the rest of their army marched to Gloucester. At my return to the rendezvous, 'twas debated at a council of war, whether to quarter in the field all night, or to march to Tewxbury; from whence we had drawn too many men: the first was resolved upon; but the enemy finding their advantage, put their garrison soldiers into boats (who were fresh) and their wearied

9

soldiers in their rooms, and surprised our garrison of Tewxbury that night; of which we had intelligence by nine the next morning.

The next forlorn-hope I was commanded upon, was with Major Sheldon, about 4 or 5 days after at Ripple-Field[1] where we did good execution upon the enemy; . . .

Caversham Fight, 25 April 1643

We were then commanded to march towards Oxon, to the relief of Reading, besieged by the Earl of Essex, with the King's whole army that quartered thereabout: where I had the honour to command the forlorn-hope[2] again; 8 or 10 days after, the general rendezvous was by Wallingford; and the forlorn-hope consisting of about 160 horse, was sent out between 8 and 9 of the clock in the morning; we marched to Nettlebed, and so to Cawsam-house; through as bad way for horse to march as ever I saw: for the way was so thick of woods and furzes, that in two miles we could not draw up 8 in front, so as a small party of horse might easily have retarded our march, and killed several of us. Our security might be the illness of the way; for none that knew not of our march before, would ever expect horse to march in that place: we saw not one scout, or armed man, till we approached Cawsam Bridge, and there we found their army prepared to entertain the King's. My station was (not directly but obliquely) between the river [*Thames*] and a large barn [*Harrison's Barn*], within musket shot of both; they sent no party out to fight us; but within half an hour the King's army appeared upon a hill, about a mile off (himself being in person there). The cannon played upon us, but did us no harm; we killed some and took others prisoners, they mistaking us for their own party: between 12 and 1 of the clock, the King sent down several regiments to storm the barn; without the taking of which, we could not have access to the body of their army, which lay mostly between the barn and the bridge: and as the King always adventured gold against silver at the best, so now he adventured as gallant men as ever drew sword, against mud walls; for the barn was as good a bulwark as art could invent. 'Twould grieve one's heart, to see men drop like ripe fruit in a strong wind, and never see their

[1] Atkyns's recollection is at fault here. Ripple Field was on 12 April, the day after Little Dean.

[2] Probably a division or squadron of the regiment consisting of two or three troops.

enemy; for they had made loopholes through the walls, that they had the full bodies of the assailants for their mark, as they came down a plain field: but the assailants saw nothing to shoot at but mud walls, and must hit them in the eye, or lose their shot. Upon this disadvantage I need not tell you what men we lost; about three of the clock, my party was relieved for half an hour, and then the party that relieved us were drawn off again.

Soon after, the King's army marched off (having relieved the town with ammunition) and my party was left as before, without hope of relief, and the sun going down; all which daunted my men so much, that I could hardly make a front of 6 men;[1] and indeed the danger was not small, for two or three hundred musketeers had lined the hedge by this time, within half musket shot of us and began to play on the one side, a regiment of foot and cannon about musket shot fronted us, and a strong party of horse on the other side; so as I had much ado to keep them from running, having a lieutenant as fearful as any; which to prevent, I was forced to cut some of them, and threaten my lieutenant; with which we stuck together more like a flock of sheep, than a party of horse; until Prince Rupert sent his commands by Colonel [*William*] Legge that I should march off, and make my retreat as well as I could; A deliverance which by the advice of that noble person, I did with such success, that I lost not one man. About half an hour within night as we marched in a broad road, my scouts discovered the enemy, and came very merrily back; at which my party took such a fright, that though I desired them with all importunity (for command was now laid asleep) that but six of them all with fixed pistols would go along with me, and I could get no more than two: by this time dragoons on both sides the road were pelting at us, but at a great distance; and a party of horse pursued us in the rear; but when they came in a convenient distance of us, we three discharged at them, and they ran away with so great a noise, that my party suspecting they had come on, ran too, but the contrary way; we were afterwards troubled with them no more: and about a quarter of a mile further, Prince Rupert had laid so strong an ambuscado for them, that if their whole army had pursued us, I'm confident he had scattered them: upon this service I was not a quarter of an hour in fourteen hours off my horse's back, and Prince Rupert declared he would never put me upon so hard duty again.

[1] Probably drawn up three deep.

The Advance to the West

Not long after, Prince Maurice his regiment with others[1] marched into the West to assist the then Marquis of Hertford[2] in raising an army in those parts (who was made General of the West) where Sir William Waller had been with his army before, to raise forces for the Parliament. Prince Maurice had such an entire affection to the King, that (not regarding his own dignity) he took a commission [*as Lieutenant-General*] under the Marquis, rather than the King's cause should fail. The Lord Carnarvan was General of the horse, and Sir James Hamilton Major General: we did not much in our march, but raise men and arms, till we came to Crock-horne, where (as I take it) we met the Lord Hopton[2] with his forces from Cornwall (having cleared those parts) which were most upon foot; this addition made us up a pretty marching army. When we came together, we were quickly upon action; but the Cornish foot could not well brook our horse (especially, when we were drawn up upon corn) but they would many times let fly at us: these were the very best foot I ever saw, for marching and fighting; but so mutinous withal, that nothing but an alarm could keep them from falling foul upon their officers.[3] The

---

[1] This force left Oxford on 15 May 1643. It included Prince Maurice's, the Earl of Carnarvon's, Colonel Thomas Howard's and Colonel Sir Humphrey Bennet's regiments of horse, and Colonel Bamfield's regiment of foot.

[2] The two armies met at Chard, not Crewkerne, on 4 June 1643. Hopton gives their strength as:

	Hertford's	Cornish	Total
Horse	1,500	500	2,000
Foot	1,000	3,000	4,000
Dragoons	—	300	300
Field pieces	10–11	4–5	14–16
Total of the two armies:			6,300

He describes Hertford's as 'new-levied', which, except for Colonel Bamfield's weak regiment, they probably were. The Cornish, he says, were 'all old soldiers' (*Bellum Civile*, p. 47).

[3] Whether or not Atkyns is exaggerating here it is only fair to compare this passage with Hopton's views at the same period: 'There [*at Taunton*] began the disorder of the horse visibly to break in upon all the prosperity of the public proceedings. The Town agreeing willingly to raise and pay £8,000 composition (which would have sufficed for some weeks necessary pay for the whole Army;) The Country being then full, and not re-lucting at free-quarter soberly taken, And the Generals being very fully advertised of the opportunity to begin a discipline in the Army, and being of themselves very desirous of

first thing that we attempted (as I remember) was the taking of Taunton Dean, which stood out at first, but when we were prepared to storm it, they yielded: I having then a commission for raising a regiment of dragoons; myself, and some of my officers went to seek for arms; of which we found many, and observing a hole in an elder hedge, I put in my hand and took out a bag of money; which if our foot had espied (who were also upon the search) they had certainly taken me for the enemy, and deprived me of both it and life.

Chewton Fight, 10 June 1643

After the garrison settled in Taunton Dean, we marched towards the enemy, who were then quartered in, and about the Bath [i.e. *the city*]; we had two very hard days' march thither: but before we came to Glastonbury, we had intelligence of some forces newly raised, marching towards their body; whom a commanded party of ours pursued, and did some execution upon: that day came Sir Horatio Carew in to us. When we came to Wells, intelligence was given us, that Sir William Waller's army was drawn out on that side of Bath; we marched toward them as far as Chuton, which I suppose, is about half way;[1] the Sun was then about an hour high, and many of our horse and foot tired with our march; so the foot had orders to quarter at Wells, as the headquarters, and the horse thereabouts: The quartermasters were sent to take up quarters accordingly; and the Lord Carnarvan with his regiment of horse, went to give their whole army an alarm; but came so near them, that for haste, they sent out a fresh regiment of horse, and another of dragoons to fight him; his Lordship's regiment being much wasted, and his horses tired with the long march, were forced to retreat; and the enemy had the pursuit of them to Chuton, where Prince Maurice was hurt, and taken prisoner. We were then a mile on our way towards our quarters,

---

it, were yet never able to represse the extravagant disorder of the horse to the ruin and discomposure of all' (*Bellum Civile*, p. 47).

If the Royalist officers had trouble to discipline their men, the root of the matter was that pay was seldom forthcoming. It is hardly strange that the soldiers were sometimes mutinous or disorderly. The wonder is that the Royalist armies managed to remain in the field for more than three years.

[1] Chewton Mendip is about five miles from Wells, and not less than twelve from Bath as the crow flies.

when Colonel Brutus Bucke acquainted our regiment with this un-
welcome news; which I heard first, having the honour to command
the rear division[1] of the regiment. My Lieutenant-Colonel [*Guy
Molesworrth*], my Major [*Thomas Sheldon*], and the rest of the officers,
advised what to do in this case; and the result was, that Prince Maurice
having himself commanded his regiment to their quarters, they were
subject to a Council of War, if they should disobey command; to
which I answered (being eldest [i.e. *senior*] captain) that I was but a
young soldier, and if they would give me leave, I would draw off
my division and run the hazard of a Council of War; they told me,
they might as well go themselves, as give me leave to go; but if I
would adventure, they would not oppose it, but defend me the best
they could.

I drew off my division with all possible speed, and put them in
order, which were not above 100 men; and before we had marched
twelve score yards, we met the Lord Carnarvan's regiment scattered,
and running so terribly, that I could hardly keep them from disorder-
ing my men (though in a large champaign) at last I met his Lordship
with his horse wellnigh spent, who told me I was the happiest sight
he ever saw in his life: I told him I was no less glad to see his Lordship; for as yet I had no command for what I had done, and now I
hoped he would give me command publicly, to preserve me from
the censures of a Council, which he did. The enemy seeing a party
make towards them left their pursuit, and drew up at Chuton, and
the Lord Carnarvan, the Lord Arundel of Wardour, with myself,
marched in the head of my party; this was about half an hour before
sunset; and when we came within 20 score of the enemy, we found
about 200 dragoons half musket shot before a regiment of horse of
theirs in two divisions, both in order to receive us. At this punctilio of
time, from as clear a sunshine day as could be seen, there fell a sudden
mist, that we could not see ten yards off, but we still marched on;
the dragoons amazed with the mist, and hearing our horse come on;
gave us a volley of shot out of distance,[2] and disordered not one man
of us, and before we came up to them, they took horse[3] and away
they run, and the mist immediately vanished. We had then the less
work to do, but still we had enough; for there were 6 troops of horse

[1] Probably his own and one other troop. Division=squadron.

[2] Distance=range.

[3] They had evidently dismounted to await the Royalists.

in 2 divisions, and about three or four hundred dragoons more, that had lined the hedges on both sides of their horse; when we came within 6 score of them, we mended our pace, and fell into their left division, routing and killing several of them.

The dragoons on both sides, seeing us so mixed with their men that they could not fire at us, but they might kill their own men as well as ours; took horse and away they run also. In this charge, I gave one Captain [*Edward*] Kitely quarter twice, and at last he was killed: the Lord Arundel of Wardour also, took a dragoon's colours,[1] as if it were hereditary to the family so to do; but all of us overran the Prince, being prisoner in that party; for he was on foot, and had a hurt upon his head,[2] and I suppose not known to be the Prince. My groom coming after us, espied the Prince, and all being in confusion, he alighted from his horse, and gave him to the Prince, which carried him off: and though this was very great success, yet we were in as great danger as ever; for now we were in disorder and had spent our shot;[3] and had not time to charge again;[4] and my Lieutenant [*Thomas Sandys*] and Cornet [*Holmes*], with above half the Party, followed the chase of those that ran, within half a mile of their army; that when I came to rally, I found I had not 30 men; we had then three fresh troops to charge, which were in our rear; but by reason of their marching through a wainshard [*waggon yard*] before they could be put in order: I told those of my party, that if we did not put a good face upon it, and charge them presently, before they were in order, we were all dead men or prisoners; which they apprehending, we charged them; and they made as it were a lane for us, being as willing to be gone as we ourselves. In this charge there was but one of my troop killed, and 8 hurt. For the wounded men of my troop, and also of my division I received 20s. a man of Sir Robert Long, then Treasurer of the Army; which was all the money I ever received for myself, or troops, during the war.

When I came to Wells, the headquarters; I was so weary that I did not my duty to the Prince that night, but laid me down where I

---

[1] His father had been 'a great Defender of the Romish Faith; not only by his Sword in taking the Turks Standard, for which he was made a German Count, but by writing for the Church of Rome' (Atkyns, p. 41).

[2] Clarendon says he received 'two shrewd hurts in the head'.

[3] Spent our shot=fired our pistols.

[4] Charge again=reload.

could get quarters; I was much unsatisfied for the loss of my Lieutenant and Colours, of which I had then no account; and laid all the
guards to give me news of them, if they escaped. Early in the morning
Mr Holmes my Cornet brought my Colours to me, which pleased
me very well; but with this allay, that my Lieutenant Thomas Sandys,
my near kinsman was taken prisoner, and one more gentleman of my
troop with him; and that he with some few troopers, took such leaps
that the enemy could not follow them, else they had been taken also.
The next morning I waited upon Prince Maurice, and presented him
with a case of pistols, which my uncle Sandys brought newly out of
France; the neatest that I ever saw, which he then wanted;[1] but as
yet he knew not the man that mounted him, nor whose horse it was:
when I saw the horse I knew him, and the man that rid him that day;
who was the groom aforesaid: the Prince told me he would not part
with the horse, till he saw the man that horsed him, if he were alive,
and commanded me to send him to him; which I did that day, and
when he came to the Prince, he knew him, and gave him 10 broad
pieces, and told him withal, that he should have any preferment he
was capable of. This graceless fellow went from my troop, and took
two troopers with him, none of which ever returned again: about
15 years after [1658?] I saw him begging in the streets of London,
with a muffler before his face, and spake inwardly, as if he had been
eaten up with the foul disease. That day I went to my quarters at
Glastonbury, where there was a handsome case of a house, but totally
plundered, and neither bread nor beer in it; but only part of a cheddar
cheese, which looking blue, I found my foot-boy giving to my grey-
hounds, and reproving him for it; he cried, saying there was nothing
else to give them: For this cheddar cheese, I was arrested in London,
which cost me £100.

'A Mad Merry Saying'

The Sunday following I desired Doctor [*John*] Cole, Prince Maurice's
Chaplain, to give me and my troop the sacrament, which he was
willing to do. That morning about 6 my Major Thomas Sheldon
called upon me, to dine with Prince Maurice; who had invited his
officers to a buck; I told him what I was to do, 'Hang't, Hang't
bully,' said he merrily 'thou may'st receive the sacrament at any time,
but thou can'st not eat venison at any time.' But that Reverend Doctor

---

[1] Presumably he had lost his the day before when he was taken prisoner.

gave me, and all my troop the communion that day; and I hope 'tis no vanity to say, this small party probably preserved the whole army, for had these two regiments carried off Prince Maurice his person, and cut off the Lord Carnarvan, and his Regiment, and given an alarm to our surbated [*exhausted*] foot, and tired horse, being divided, I know not what had become of us. There was one, intituled [*sic*] to this action (which was usual in the King's army) whom I am sure never struck [*a*] stroke in it, (but was within distance to have fallen into the rear of the last three troops, and to have helped us if he would) but there being no good understanding between Prince Maurice and Marquis Hertford's regiments,[1] their chaplains and secretaries, whose places were not to fight, or to be in the field; gave seldom true intelligence, but rather as their affections lead them, supposing that if such things were done, they must be done by such and such persons.

'The Battle of Tog-Hill', Lansdown, 5 June 1643

After we had refreshed ourselves about a week in quarters, we began to seek out the enemy, who were not far off; for four or five days, we skirmished by parties every day, and kept our body close together expecting battle daily. Each army consisting of about 6,000 horse and foot, but theirs thought to be most; our headquarters were Marsh-field,[2] theirs Bath, within five miles of each other: very early in the morning we sent out a party of horse, about 300, commanded by a Major,[3] who did it so ill, that encouraged the enemies' forlorn-hope to advance so far, as to give a strong alarm to our whole army; and we were forced to draw out in haste: the ground we stood in, was like a straight horn, about six score yards over at the end towards Marshfield, and twenty score over at the end towards their army; on both sides enclosed with a hedge, and woods without that. They stood upon a high hill which commanded us, that opened to a large down, from whence they could discover our motions, but we could not theirs; both bodies within two miles of each other. For four or five

---

[1] Atkyns seems to be getting at some officer of Hertford's regiment of horse. *Mercurius Aulicus* says that Captain Stowell 'with some part of the Lord Marquesse his Regiment;' took part in this charge. Perhaps Atkyns is referring to him.

[2] Hopton gives a good account of the manoeuvres between Chewton Fight and the battle of Lansdown, a period of which Atkyns says nothing.

[3] Major George Lower of Colonel Thomas Howard's regiment of horse, who was killed at Lansdown.

hours, we sent parties out of each body to skirmish, where I think we had the better; but about 3 of the clock they (seeing their advantage) sent down a strong party of horse, commanded by Colonel [*Robert*] Burrell, Major [*Jonas*] Vantruske and others; not less than 300, and five or six hundred dragoons on both sides of the hedges, to make way for their advance, and to make good their retreat. And this was the boldest thing that I ever saw the enemy do; for a party of less than 1000 to charge an army of 6000 horse, foot and cannon, in their own ground, at least a mile and a half from their body.

Our horse being placed before our foot and cannon, were commanded off troop by troop; and being within half musket shot of the hedges lined on both sides by their dragoons; several horses were killed, and some of our men; their muskets playing very hard upon our horse, made us retreat so disorderly, that they fell foul upon our foot; and indeed there was not room enough for us to retreat in order, unless we had gone upon the very mouths of their muskets: I suppose the stratagem was to draw on their party of horse upon our foot and cannon, the better to rout them, and then our horse to fall in upon them to do execution; for the dragoons making their way by pioneers, were not discovered till they shot. Our commanders seeing the army in such disorder, and the enemies' horse marching near us; commanded the then Marquis Hertford's Lifeguard of horse[1] to charge them, who never charged before; which was then commanded by that honourable and loyal person the Lord Arundell of Trerice: I seeing all like to have been lost, unless a sudden check were given to this party of horse; desired him to give me leave to charge with him, with these words, 'That we would answer for one another that day': we charged together, and both of us fell upon the commander-in-chief [*Colonel Robert Burrill*], and hurt him so, that he reeled and wheeled off, and the party with him; there were several others hurt and killed on each side, of the Marquis' Lifeguard Mr Lee and Mr Barker, gentlemen of quality.

'Twas now no time to draw out a party of commanded men,[2] but the Lord Carnarvan (according to his usual course) drew up his regiment as soon as possible, and pursued them almost to their body, and killed and took several prisoners; in which charge (or soon after) he had a shot in the leg, that disabled him for further service at that time.

[1] Probably about fifty or sixty strong, the average strength of a troop.

[2] That is to say a few from each troop.

The enemy to encourage us to persecute this success, gave all the symptoms of a flying army; as blowing up of powder, horse and foot running distractedly upon the edge of the hill, for we could see no further: these signs made Sir Robert Welsh importunately desire the Prince to have a party to follow the chase, which he gave him the command of, and me of the reserve; but when he came up the hill, and saw in what order they lay, he soon quit his employment there; and desired he might have my command and I his, which was ordered accordingly. As I went up the hill, which was very steep and hollow, I met several dead and wounded officers brought off; besides several running away, that I had much ado to get up by them. When I came to the top of the hill, I saw Sir Bevill Grinvill's stand of pikes, which certainly preserved our army from a total rout, with the loss of his most precious life: they stood as upon the eaves of an house for steepness, but as unmovable as a rock; on which side of this stand of pikes our horse were, I could not discover; for the air was so darkened by the smoke of the powder, that for a quarter of an hour together (I dare say) there was no light seen, but what the fire of the volleys of shot gave; and 'twas the greatest storm that ever I saw, in which though I knew not whither to go, nor what to do, my horse had two or three musket bullets in him presently, which made him tremble under me at that rate, and I could hardly with spurs keep him from lying down; but he did me the service to carry me off to a led horse, and then died: by that time I came up to the hill again, the heat of the battle was over, and the sun set, but still pelting at one another half musket shot off: the enemy had a huge advantage of ground upon our men, for their foot were in a large sheep-cot, which had a stone wall about it as good a defence against any thing but cannon as could be, and ours upon the edge of the hill, so steep that they could hardly draw up; 'tis true there were shelves near the place like Romish [*Roman*] works, where we quartered that night, but so shallow that my horse had a bullet in his neck: we pelted at one another till half an hour before day, and then we heard not any noise, but saw light matches upon the wall, which our commanders observing, sent one to discover whether they had quit the field or not, who brought news that they were gone.

There were killed of officers that day, Sir Bevill Grinvill, Major [*George*] Lower, Lieutenant Colonel [*Joseph*] Wall, &c. Hurt, the Lord Carnarvan, Colonel [*Sir Humphrey*] Bennett, &c. and several other officers taken prisoners, and more than all these ran away to Oxon, to carry tidings of our defeat before it was. At the Council of

War that night, were Prince Maurice, the Lord Hopton, Sir James Hamilton, Major Sheldon, and some others; the result of that Council was, that if the enemy fell upon us, every man to shift for himself: in order to which, the cannon were drawn off; so that this battle was so hard fought on both sides, that they forsook the field first, and we had leave so to do. The next morning was very clear, and about half an hour after sun rising, we rendezvoused our horse and foot upon Togge-Hill, between the hill where we quartered all night, and Marshfield; Major Sheldon and myself, went towards the Lord Hopton, who was then viewing the prisoners taken, some of which, were carried upon a cart wherein was our ammunition; and (as I heard) had match to light their tobacco; the Major desired me to go back to the regiment, whilst he received orders of his Lordship: I had no sooner turned my horse, and was gone 3 horses lengths from him, but the ammunition was blown up, and the prisoners in the cart with it; together with the Lord Hopton, Major Sheldon, and Cornet Washnage, who was near the cart on horseback, and several others: it made a very great noise, and darkened the air for a time, and the hurt men made lamentable screeches. As soon as the air was clear, I went to see what the matter was; there I found his Lordship miserably burnt, his horse singed like parched leather, and Thomas Sheldon (that was a horse lengths further from the blast) complaining that the fire was got within his breeches, which I tore off as soon as I could, and from as long a flaxen head of hair as ever I saw, in the twinkling of an eye, his head was like a blackamoor; his horse was hurt, and run away like mad, so that I put him upon my horse, and got two troopers to hold him up on both sides, and bring him to the headquarters, whilst I marched after with the regiment.

The enemy (having intelligence of this disaster, and also a recruit that night of fresh men) gave us no time to repair our losses; but marched up to our headquarters, before we could bury our dead, or make provision to secure our wounded; but Washnage died and gave me his charging horse, which I much wanted; the rest (which were many) were provided for, either in the Marquis' coach, or litters made with boards, except Major Thomas Sheldon, who was left to the mercy of the enemy; which he perceiving made shift to get to the rendezvous, and when he found there was nothing but a cart provided for him, what with the cold he took, but rather I think, out of the magnanimity of his courage, as soon as he was put in there, he immediately died; by whose death I lost my martial mistress [*patron*], but had not time to bewail it; whose death when the Prince heard of, he sent several officers to bring me to him, and gave me his place[1] publicly in the field, with the greatest honour and kindness imaginable: I was also that day made Adjutant General of the Army.

The Retreat to Devizes, 6 June 1643

The foot and cannon (by the loss of ammunition) became wholly unserviceable to us. The enemy pursued, and we were to make our retreat to Devizes, otherwise called the Vies; Lieutenant Colonel [*Richard*] Nevill was commanded to bring up the rear, which he did with that gallantry, and good conduct, that we killed as many of the enemy as they did of us; when the foot came safe to the Vies, and that the Horse had only done that service; instead of calling us runaway horse (which the Cornish used to do) they called us gallant horse; for the Cornish foot knew not till then the service of horse.[2] When we came to the Vies, there was found (as I heard) two barrels of powder, and the bellropes [*bedropes*] made matches; and 'twas fortified as well as it was capable of, in a short time. While our army was in and about the Vies, our scouts gave no satisfactory account for several hours where the enemy was; whereupon Sir James Hamilton[3] commanded me personally to seek out the enemy and give a certain account where they were, or never to return again: 'Twas my good fortune in less than half an hour to fire at one of their scouts, and by his flight to discover their whole body, of which I gave full satisfaction.

The enemy made no near approaches to the town, nor did they storm it on any part; our horse being still in a condition to give them a charge: Sir James Hamilton gave me the honour and trust to quarter our horse where I thought fit, giving him an account (at the Council of War, whither he was then going) what I had done: after I had quartered them in a very convenient place, I went to the Council of War; where I found the general officers, and some few more at supper; Prince Maurice asked me whether I had quartered the horse

[1] Major of the regiment.

[2] Atkyns is exaggerating here. Major Walter Slingsby, of Lord Mohun's regiment of foot, fought a stubborn rearguard action during this retreat (Hopton).

[3] It will be recalled that Carnarvon, the Lieutenant-General of the horse, had been wounded; Hamilton as Major-General now commanded the horse.

well, and I told him I had; he bid me say no more but sit down to supper, after supper, all but the general officers and some others withdrew, and I gave my account and afterwards proferred to withdraw, but I was permitted to stay; and after the Council resolved what to do, I was commanded to draw up the horse into the market-place, where Sir James Hamilton received them.

The Retreat of the Horse to Oxford

About midnight, our horse marched, or rather made an escape out of town, leaving the foot behind us; we met not the enemy at all, but some of our own forces, whose fears scattered them, and we were like to fall foul upon each other: they were part of the horse that should have come to our assistance, but hearing ill news secured themselves, viz. the Lord Craffords regiment, between three and four hundred, and Colonel James Long's regiment, between two and three hundred. At the break of day, we were at least 8 miles from the Vies,[1] and free from all enemies between that and Oxon; Prince Maurice and several of the officers galloped to Oxon,[2] to be there as soon as they could; but my horse had cast two shoes, and I was forced to stay behind to set them at Lambourne, where leaning against a post, I was so sleepy that I fell down like a log of wood, and could not be awakened for half an hour: 'twas impossible then to overtake them; so I went to Farringdon, being not able to reach Oxford that Night; I fell off my horse back twice upon the downs, before I came to Farringdon, where I reeled upon my horse so extremely that the people of the town took me to be dead drunk: when I came to my house (for there I sometimes lived) I despatched a man and horse presently to the Prince to receive orders, and desired my wife's aunt to provide a bed for me; the good woman took me to be drunk too, and provided a bed for me presently, where I slept at least fourteen hours together without waking.

The Battle of Roundway Down, 13 July 1643

The next morning[3] I had orders that the rendezvous was about

[1] About Beckhampton, presumably.

[2] He arrived at Oxford on the afternoon of 11 July, and started back the next day, with Sir John Byron's brigade (*Mercurius Aulicus*, p. 367).

[3] Apparently 12 July.

Marlborough, whither I went with several horse quartered at Farringdon,[1] and came timely thither: the Lord Wilmot was sent with a recruit of horse from Oxon, and I suppose all the horse at that rendezvous were about 1800 and two small pieces of cannon: we lost no time, but marched towards the enemy, who stood towards the top of the hill; the foot in the middle between two wings of horse, and the cannon before the foot: there were four hills like the four corners of a die, in such a champaign, as 40,000 men might fight in. Upon one of the hills[2] we discharged our cannon, to give notice to our foot that we were come to their relief: then forlorn-hopes out of each army were drawn out, and the Lord Wilmott's Major, Paul Smith commanded ours, who did it with that gallantry, that he beat them into the very body of their left wing, and put them out of order; which we took advantage of, and immediately charged the whole body; the charge was so sudden that I had hardly time to put on my arms, we advanced a full trot 3 deep, and kept in order; the enemy kept their station, and their right wing of horse being cuirassiers, were I'm sure five, if not six deep, in so close order, that Punchinello himself had he been there, could not have gotten in to them.

All the horse on the left hand of Prince Maurice his regiment, had none to charge; we charging the very utmost man of their right wing: I cannot better compare the figure of both armies than to the map of the fight at sea, between the English and the Spanish Armadas, (only there was no half moon) for though they were above twice our numbers; they being six deep, in close order and we but three deep, and open (by reason of our sudden charge) we were without them at both ends: the cannoneers seeing our resolution, did not fire their cannon. No men ever charged better than ours did that day, especially the Oxford horse, for ours were tired and scattered, yet those that were there did their best.

My Engagement with Sir Arthur Haslerigge

'Twas my fortune in a direct line to charge their general of horse [*Sir Arthur Hesilrige*], which I supposed to be so by his place; he discharged his carbine first, but at a distance not to hurt us, and afterwards one of his pistols, before I came up to him, and missed with

---

[1] Faringdon, Berkshire, seventeen miles from Oxford, was one of the ring of royalist garrisons which formed the outer defence of that city.

[2] Roughridge hill.

both: I then immediately struck into him, and touched him before I discharged mine; and I'm sure I hit him, for he staggered, and presently wheeled off from his party and ran.

Here I must desire the readers to be very particular in this relation, because twenty several persons have entitled themselves to this action and a Knight[1] that shall be nameless, that is dead (speaking of his great services and small rewards to me) told me the very ensuing story himself, all but that he could not give so good reason as I could, why it was Sir Arthur Haslerigge. When he wheeled off, I pursued him, and had not gone twenty yards after him, but I heard a voice saying, "Tis Sir Arthur Haslerigge follow him'; but from which party the voice came I knew not they being joined, nor never did know till about seven years since, but follow him I did, and in six score yards I came up to him, and discharged the other pistol at him, and I'm sure I hit his head, for I touched it before I gave fire, and it amazed him at that present, but he was too well armed all over for a pistol bullet to do him any hurt, having a coat of mail over his arms and a headpiece (I am confident) musket proof, his sword had two edges and a ridge in the middle, and mine [was] a strong tuck;[2] after I had slackened my pace a little, he was gone twenty yards from me, riding three quarters speed, and down the side of a hill, his posture was waving his sword on the right and left hand of his horse, not looking back [to see] whether he were pursued or not, (as I conceive) to daunt any horse that should come up to him; [in] about six score more I came up to him again (having a very swift horse that Cornet Washnage gave me) and stuck by him a good while, and tried him from head to the saddle, and could not penetrate him, nor do him any hurt; but in this attempt he cut my horse's nose, that you might put your finger in the wound, and gave me such a blow on the inside of my arm amongst the veins that I could hardly hold my sword; he went on as before, and I slackened my pace again, and found my horse drop blood, and not so bold as before; but about eight score more I got up to him again, thinking to have pulled him off his horse; but he having now found the way, struck my horse upon the cheek, and cut off half the headstall of my bridle, but falling off from him, I ran his horse into the body and resolved to attempt nothing further than to kill his horse; all this time we were together hand to fist.

[1] Possibly Sir Robert Welsh.

[2] A long, straight, heavy cavalry sword.

In this nick of time came up Mr Holmes[1] to my assistance, (who never failed me in time of danger) and went up to him with great resolution, and felt him before he discharged his pistol, and though I saw him hit him, 'twas but a flea-biting to him; whilst he charged him, I employed myself in killing his horse, and ran him into several places, and upon the faltering of his horse his headpiece opened behind, and I gave him a prick in the neck, and I had run him through the head if my horse had not stumbled at the same place; then came in Captain Buck[2] a gentleman of my troop, and discharged his pistol upon him also, but with the same success as before, and being a very strong man, and charging with a mighty hanger,[3] stormed him and amazed him, but fell off again; by this time his horse began to be faint with bleeding, and fell off from his rate, at which said Sir Arthur, 'What good will it do you to kill a poor man?' said I 'Take quarter then', with that he stopped his horse, and I came up to him, and bid him deliver his sword, which he was loathe to do; and being tied twice about his wrist, he was fumbling a great while before he would part with it; but before he delivered it, there was a runaway troop of theirs that had espied him in hold; says one of them 'My Lord General is taken prisoner'; says another, 'Sir Arthur Haslerigge is taken prisoner, face about and charge', with that they rallied and charged us, and rescued him; wherein I received a shot with a pistol, which only took off the skin upon the blade bone of my shoulder.

This story being related to the late King [*Charles I*] at a second, or third hand, his answer was, 'Had he been victualled as well as fortified, he might have endured a siege of seven years, &c.' His horse died in the place, and they horsed him upon another, and went away together. 'Twas one of the best horses the late King had at the Mews he rid upon, and 'twas the late King's saddle, which I had; and when I went to the Parliament quarters, I gave it to Sir Henry Wroth: When we came back to the army (which in so confused a field was difficult to do) we found the enemies' foot still in a close body, their muskets lined with pikes, and fronting every way, expecting their horse to rally and come to their relief; in the mean time our horse charged them, but to no purpose, they could not get into them, at last, when they saw our foot march from the Vies, and come within a mile of

1 Atkyns's cornet.

2 Presumably a reformado officer.

3 Hanger—a kind of cutlass.

them, they asked quarter, and threw down their arms in a moment:[1] we lost few men (especially of quality) and they many; Sir James Hamilton was very much hurt, and Lieutenant-Colonel Molesworth my Lieutenant-Colonel, who went to Oxford; by whose absence I commanded the regiment in chief: when I alighted I found my horse had done bleeding, his cuts being upon the gristly part of his nose, and the cheek near the bone; I bade my groom have a great care of him, and go into quarters immediately; but instead . . . this rogue went directly to Oxford, left my hurt horse at Marlborough with a farrier, and sold another barb[2] of mine at Oxon, and carried my portmanteau with him into the North which had all my clothes and linen in it, and other things worth above £100, and I never saw him more: my charging horse I had again, and some money for my barb, which was bought at an under value, being no good title: but for want of a shift (my wound having bloodied my linen) I became so lousy in three or four days, that I could not tell what to do with myself; and when I had got a shift, which was not till we took Bath; my blood, and the sweat of my body had so worn it, that it fell off into lint.

'Prince Maurice His Kind Intentions Towards Me'

Soon after the prisoners and trophies and the matters of the field were disposed of, a Council of War was called at the Vies, and Prince Maurice sent for me thither to attend him, as soon as I was come he had notice and came out to me, and bade me wait there, telling me, that he intended to send the Trophies and Letters to the King by me; but upon comparison of commissions, 'twas found that the Lord Wilmott was commander in chief for that expedition, who sent Sir

---

[1] The Parliamentarian army at Roundway Down consisted of:

5 regiments of foot	1,800–2,500
6 regiments of horse	2,000
1 regiment of dragoons	500
7–9 brass cannon	
	———
	5,000

Waller lost 600 killed, and 800–1,200 prisoners, besides 7 cannon. The Royalists took 28 ensigns and 8 or 9 cornets.

[2] Barb—a horse of the Barbary breed, remarkable for speed, endurance and docility.

Robert Welsh, and I returned to my quarters.[1] After we were refreshed in our quarters, we marched to Bath; which town the enemy
had newly quitted, and marched, or rather retreated to Bristoll; there
I found my Lieutenant Thomas Sandys, formerly taken prisoner,
recovering of his wounds, but not well able to go abroad: we were
very glad to see each other, and I desired him to tell me the manner
of his being taken; he told me, he pursued the enemy too near their
body, and they sent out fresh horse upon him and took him, and gave
him quarter without asking; but after he was their prisoner, a Scot
shot him into the body with two pistol bullets, which were still in
him, so that he was very near death: when he was brought to the
town, Sir William Waller enquiring what prisoners were taken,
heard of his name, and came to see him; he seemed exceeding angry
at the inhumane action that befel him, and sent for his own chirurgeon
immediately, and saw him dressed before he went away; he gave the
innkeeper charge that he should have whatever he called for, and he
would see him paid; that whatsoever woman he sent for to attend
him, should be admitted, and lent him ten broad pieces for his own
private expenses; and before he marched to Bristoll, he came to see
him again, and finding him not able to march, took his parole, to
render himself a true prisoner to him at Bristoll when he was able
to ride; which I found (for his word sake) he was inclinable to do; to
which I answered that he was now made free by as good authority
as took him prisoner, and that I expected he should return to his
command; upon which we struck a heat and at last referred the
business to the Lord Carnarvan to determine.

A Case in War Determined

The case was agreed to be 'whether a prisoner upon his parole to
render himself to the enemy, being afterwards redeemed by his own
party, ought to keep his parole or not'. His Lordship heard arguments
on both sides; at last said thus, that there had been lately a precedent
in the Council of War in a case of like nature, wherein it was resolved,
that if the prisoner (being redeemed by a martial power without any
consent of his own) shall afterwards refuse the command he was in
before and attempt to render himself prisoner to the enemy, he shall

[1] There is little doubt that, had Atkyns been sent, he would have been knighted, as were
Sir Richard Crane after Powick Bridge, Sir John Urry after Chalgrove Field, and Sir
Thomas Gardiner after the relief of Newark.

be taken as an enemy, and be kept prisoner by his own party; the reason seems very strong because he may be prevailed upon by the enemy to betray his own party; and the freeing of his person, gives him as it were a new election; and if he choose rather to be a prisoner than a free man; it demonstrates his affection to be there. But this did not satisfy my Lieutenant, for he would not take his place as before, but marched along with the troop as my prisoner, till the taking of Bristoll (the place where he promised to render himself) and then he thought he was fully absolved from his parole, and betook himself to his employment again.

The Taking of Bristol, 26 July 1643

When we came to Bristoll, Prince Rupert (whose very name was half a conquest) with the Oxford Army lay before it on the West side, and Prince Maurice with the Western Army on the East: both armies being not half enough to besiege it; our Cornish foot were to fall on first, which they performed with a great deal of gallantry and resolution; but it proving the stronger part of the town, they were beaten off, with a great deal of loss; when they found it inaccessible, they got carts laden with faggots, to fill up the 'graft'; but it being so deep, and full of water (though they attempted it again very gallantly) they could do no good upon it; but as gallant men as ever drew sword (pardon the comparison) lay upon the ground like rotten sheep: amongst which were slain Colonel Brutus Buck, Sir Nicolas Slaning,[1] Colonel [John] Trevanion, with many more; howsoever this loss of ours drew the town forces that way, which might be some advantage to Prince Rupert's forces, who stormed that part of the town with such irresistible courage, that forced them from their works, and gave admission to the horse; who soon beat them from their guards, and took the town by ... which, the West was upon the matter cleared, for this gave such a reputation to our army, that made all the garrisons thereabouts willing to come in upon terms, as Dorchester and Poole [August] came in to the Lord Carnarvan, who was sent with a party of less than 1,000 men, to demand them; both (of) which [sur]rendered within one week. I cannot tell whether the articles[2] were too large; but I too much fear the not strictly performing them, did moulder

---

[1] Printed as Sir William Slaning, but corrected in an old-fashioned hand.

[2] The articles for the surrender of Bristol.

two gallant armies; the one before Lime,[1] the other before Gloucester [*10 August–5 September*] that otherwise might have come in; which had they taken or the Field Army marched up to London, to have joined with the Marquis of Newcastle, who was then successful in the North; there had been probably, an end of the war on the King's side; but this is not to the purpose in hand, for which I ask pardon, and return to myself.

The Siege of Gloucester, 10 August–5 September 1643

When we were possessed of Bristoll, and the lesser garrisons came tumbling in to the obedience of the King, I took the King's crown to be settled upon his head again; and my place of Major to the Prince, being supplied by a more knowing officer [*Major Robert Legge*] I desired leave to return to my private condition as before, and to march with the army that was to besiege Gloucester, hoping to possess my estate there; offering my lieutenant, cornet, and several other gentlemen the command of my troop, all which refused to serve in my place; so that it ceased to be a troop, and became a little army, for in less than a week, I preferred twenty of them to be captains, lieutenants and cornets.

'My Wife's Unhappy Journey to London'

After the siege of Gloucester was raised, the Parliament that were very low before, began to prick up their ears again; and I retired to Oxford, where I was offered several very good commands, but refused them all: at length money began to grow short, and my wife's estate and mine, were chiefly in the Parliament quarters; my wife therefore went up to London to make money, there being several hackney coaches come down with the commissioners, which were to treat at Oxford which had the Parliament's pass, to go up and down; by which means, I thought she might go safely; yet I endeavoured to get a pass of the Lord General [*Lord Forth*] also, but could not obtain it so soon as the coach was to return; so she adventured without a pass, which proved very unhappy, for at Nettlebed, a party of Sir Jacob Ashley's soldiers (who was then Governor of Reading) took

[1] Prince Maurice did not lay siege to Lyme until March 1644. At the time Atkyns is speaking of he was really occupied before Plymouth.

her prisoner, and carried her to Reading, where the waters being then over high, she took a great fright. When she was brought to Reading, young Sir John Cademan asked the soldiers who she was, and when he understood she was my wife, he used her with all the respect that could be, and waited on her to the Governor, who for my sake expressed many civilities to her and sent a guard with her into the Parliament quarters.

When she came to London, she found her house [*in the Strand*] full of soldiers, and could not be admitted there, but lodged at the house of one of her tenants that joined to it; where seeing her goods carried away before her face, and finding her uncle (who was possessed of her estate) inhumanly unkind to her, she fell ill and miscarried (as I understood) of three children, and was very near her death; yet in this sickness she sent a token to me, by a kinsman to Oxford, and desired a lock of my hair, which she had.

After, I thought fit to remove to Bristoll, and she unsatisfied with my absence, sent a gentlewoman of quality to see how I did there; who was forced to go the greatest part of the way on foot, the war being then so hot, that men could not travel. After half a year's stay at Bristoll, I came to Oxford again, towards the Treaty of Uxbridge [*January–February 1645*]; whither the King sent me with letters to his commissioners: my wife retiring thereabouts for air, heard of it, and came to me, but yet so weak, that when she alighted out of the coach, she fell into a swoon . . .: there I stayed as long as the treaty lasted; being the very last messenger that was sent back to Oxford. . . .

'The King's Gracious Advice'

After that treaty I stayed not long at Oxford, having no employment in the army; but asked the King's leave to go up to London, who did not only give me his free leave, but withal; directions . . . to this effect, viz.:

'I know you are too much a gentleman, and my friend, to do me any prejudice; and if you will do me any good, it must be by getting money in your purse: I know there will be those that will arise in my behalf, but they will be so small and insignificant, that it will but establish my enemies the better; by no means join with them, but the time will come, in which my people will return to their obedience; and though perhaps I may never see it myself, I am confident my son shall.'

And so gave me his hand to kiss, and the Lord of Bristoll then Secretary gave me a pass, and Colonel [*William*] Legg, then Governor of Oxford, gave me direction which way to go, having also a pass from the Speaker[1] of Parliament.

'A Challenge'

. . . I have ever . . . avoided duels as much as in honour I could (rather to preserve a good conscience, than an ill carcase) yet some I have been very near, of which I will only name one.

In Oxford, a Knight provoked me with so ill language, that I could not forbear striking of him; and being very angry, I took his periwig off from his head and trampled it under my feet: the next morning he sent me a challenge by his second, a person of quality, who found me in bed: I desired him to stay a little, and I would send for my second, to go along with him to his friend, which he did; when I sent my servant for my second, I also commanded him to secure a good charging horse by the way (intending to fight him on horseback); in less than half an hour, my second and servant came to me, and then (having the privilege to choose time, place and weapon) I told him I would meet his friend and himself, with this gentleman my second, on horseback in Bullington Green, between two and three of the clock that afternoon, with sword and pistols, and without arms,[2] and showed him my sword and pistols; saying withal, I would not except against any his friend should bring; which he desired me to send in writing, and I did it by mine own second, who brought me word back, that all was well accepted: we all dined together with other company (as we used to do) without any suspicion of a quarrel, that I know of, after dinner, my second and I mounted, and as we passed by Magdalen College (which was the way to the place appointed) the second on the other side, called to my second, desiring to speak with him, his business was to persuade me to alight, and treat of the matter in his chamber there; they both entreated me to alight, assuring me 'twas not dishonourable, . . . but I not convinced by their arguments, utterly refused, unless the principal himself would come and desire it, and absolve me from my promise of meeting him at the place appointed; which he did, and then we went up together

[1] William Lenthall (1591–1662).

[2] That is without defensive armour, such as back, breast or pot.

to his second's chamber, where we found an Earl (whose sister the Knight had married) who also pretended friendship to me; he urged how much I was beforehand with his brother, and proposed . . . that I should declare I was sorry for it, which I desired to be excused in; at last he offered that if I would say I was sorry for what I had done, he should say he was sorry for giving the occasion; which was acknowledged on both sides, and so we were made friends.

'The Cruelty of those Times'

From Oxford, the first night I came to Uxbridge [*forty miles*], where I thought fit to acquaint the governor of the town with my condition, lest I should be taken as a spy; but notwithstanding my pass (to show his officiousness to the Parliament) he carried me prisoner to London, where I was forced to make friends to the Speaker to be released: soon after, I attended my composition[1] at Goldsmiths-Hall, where (though I was a prisoner to the Parliament) yet my creditor arrested me upon an execution, and carried me away to the Poultry Compter, and then sequestered my whole estate; which if he had done before, might have paid him half his debt. There I stayed about a year without seeing a yard of growing grass; striving to be released upon the privilege of Parliament, being their prisoner; but that failing me, I removed to the King's Bench where (the Lady Lenthall being my kinswoman) I had convenient liberty: whilst I was in prison, my wife agitated my composition,[2] raised money and paid it, and I wanted not . . .

[1] The settling of his debts.

[2] Atkyns was originally fined £500 on 29 January 1646. On 23 March this was reduced to £140, of which £50 was to be paid at once and the rest in three months (*Calendar of the Committee for Compounding*, Part II, p. 1086).

Appendix I

THE SERVICES OF PRINCE MAURICE'S REGIMENT
OF HORSE

1642

23 Sept.	Fight at Powick Bridge
23 Oct.	Battle of Edgehill
9 Dec.	Quartered at Faringdon

1643

2 Feb.	Storming of Cirencester
11 Apr.	Fight at Little Dean
12 Apr.	Fight at Ripple Field
25 Apr.	Caversham Fight
10 June	Chewton Fight
5 July	Battle of Lansdown
13 July	Battle of Roundway Down
26 July	Storming of Bristol (about 200 strong)
Aug.	Siege of Gloucester (400 strong)
20 Sept.	First battle of Newbury

1644

29 Mar.	Battle of Cheriton
10 Apr.	Rendezvous at Auborne Chase (7 troops, 300 strong)
29 June	Battle of Cropredy Bridge (Cornish campaign)
27 Oct.	Second battle of Newbury
9 Nov.	Relief of Donnington Castle

1645

30 May	Siege of Leicester (150 strong)
14 June	Battle of Naseby

1646

14 Jan.	Quarters beaten up at Tudbury

Appendix II

Horse	*Foot*	
Colonels	Colonels	
Prince Maurice	Sir Bevil Grenvile	⎫
Earl of Carnarvon	Sir Nicholas Slanning	⎪
Thomas Howard	John Trevanion	⎬ Cornish
Sir Humphrey Bennet	William Godolphin	⎪
Sir James Hamilton	Lord Mohun	⎭
Marquis of Hertford	Joseph Bamfield	
Marquis of Hertford's Lifeguard	Marquis of Hertford	
Sir George Vaughan	Prince Maurice	
Sir Ralph Hopton	Brutus Buck	
	Sir Ralph Hopton	

There were ten foot regiments in the Western Army. The best were the five Cornish regiments of volunteers which had been raised in 1642 and had driven the Parliamentarians out of Cornwall and Devon. They were experienced troops, who had distinguished themselves at Bradock Down (19 January 1643), and Stratton (16 May).

Of the other five, four were new regiments levied during Hertford's westward march, while the other was a weak regiment under Colonel Bamfield, which had accompanied the Marquis from Oxford in order to guard his train of artillery.

Bamfield's did not take part in the storming of Bristol (26 July) and nor did Hopton's, though it was certainly being raised in June. The rest were all at Bristol.

Appendix III

Colonel	*Brigadier*
Lieutenant-General Lord Wilmot	Wilmot
Lord Digby	Wilmot
Sir John Digby[1]	Wilmot[2] (probably)
Sir John Byron	Byron
Henry? Sandys	Byron
Earl of Crawford	Crawford
James Long	Crawford
Thomas Morgan	Unknown
Prince Maurice	Unknown

So far as is known all the colonels of these regiments, with the exception of Lord Digby, were present in person.

[1] According to *Hector Britannicus* Sir John Digby's regiment fought Hesilrige's Lobsters, therefore he must have been in Wilmot's brigade. (See Byron's account in *Journal of Army Historical Research*, 1953.)

[2] On 11 July Secretary Nicholas wrote to Rupert saying that Wilmot, with six regiments of horse, was going back with Maurice to the West (Warburton, II, p. 227), but according to *Mercurius Aulicus* (p. 365) on 10 July there were only three regiments in Lord Wilmot's brigade. The other three must have been in Byron's brigade.

John Gwyn

Introduction

The literature of the Great Civil War includes the reminiscences of several generals. The *Military Memoirs of Captain John Gwyn* are exceptional (though not quite unique) inasmuch as they present the conflict as seen through the eyes of a Royalist company commander. The presentation, moreover, is as novel as the writer's ingenuous views.

Even the history of the *Memoirs* is unusual. This remarkable collection of papers made its appearance fortuitously in Ireland, having found its way into the home of the Rev. John Grahame of Lifford near Strabane. Realizing the manuscript's worth, the clergyman sent it to Sir Walter Scott, who edited it. In 1822 these reminiscences appeared in book form, being jointly published by Hurst, Robinson and Co of London and Archibald Constable and Co, Edinburgh. This quarto volume is now rare. John Gwyn would have remained in the ranks of unknown Civil War officers had he not wielded his quill as adroitly as his sword. He lives again in these pages.

Who was John Gwyn? His only portrait is the word picture he unconsciously paints of himself. Unannounced the young man strides on to the stage of history, experiences many vicissitudes and then with equal suddenness vanishes. But in this absorbing glimpse it is possible to catch a vision of the typical 'Cavalier': devoted, courageous, cheerful, indomitable and always debonair. His occasional gasconades may be pardoned.

John Gwyn came from Trelydan in Montgomeryshire. His father was Robert Gywn, gentleman, son of Edmund Gwyn, barrister-at-law of Gray's Inn, and Catherine, daughter of Oliver Price of Forden in Shropshire. Proud of his ancestry, Gwyn traces his descent from Cadogan ap Bleddin, Prince of Powys, and from Brochwell, King of Powys and Earl of Chester, who lived *c.* A.D. 600.[1] Sir Charles Lloyd, the second colonel under whom Gwyn served, could boast a similar descent.

How Gwyn came to be at Court is not explained, but in one of

---

[1] His lengthy and somewhat mythological family tree, published in Scott's edition, is here omitted.

his prefatory letters[1] he mentions that as a young man he spent several years under the management of the Board of Green Cloth. He informs the recipients that he was 'bred in the nursery of your yong clearks at Court'. Whatever his official post was it seems clear that he instructed the Royal children in military and physical exercises, and participated in their drill parades. He makes mention of his prowess as a pole-vaulter, asserting that he owed his life at the First Battle of Newbury to 'that Exercise which your Majesty [*Charles II*], in your junior years, was so often pleased to command me to practice before you'.

Perhaps the most puzzling aspect of these peculiar *Memoirs* is *why* they were written. At first they appear to be a memorial to support the writer's application for promotion. 'He seems to have been passed over in the course of promotion in the Royal Guards, where he had so long been an officer,' writes Scott, in his Introduction, 'and to have been left to embarrassment, if not to want.'

Though Gwyn scorns dates, internal evidence suggests that the *Memoirs* were penned between 1679 and 1682—certainly at a period when the writer was getting on in years. He claims to be entitled to be major of the Royal Regiment of Guards, an appointment which (according to the Army List of 1661) had then been more suitably filled by Colonel Henry Washington, a veteran who had been Governor of Worcester in the first Civil War. Could Gwyn have cherished any genuine hope of obtaining such a post?

Though Gwyn had been an officer in the Royal Regiment of Guards at the Restoration, he had apparently been deprived of his commission, as in 1663 the name of John Gwyn, captain of foot, appears in *A List of [Indigent] Officers*, under the Earl of Holland, with whom he had served in the uprising of 1648. But although he was no longer an officer in the Royal Regiment, he seems to have continued to serve, presumably as a gentleman trooper under the Duke of Monmouth.

If there was no prospect of his becoming major, what could have induced him to undertake the laborious task of preparing these *Memoirs*? Was it a sop to his pride? An outlet for frustrated ambition? The answer is not easy to find. Copies of the *Memoirs* were sent to eleven patrons. This task alone testifies to his tenacity, yet his appeals seem to have fallen on deaf ears.

[1] See Appendix, p. 104.

Sir Walter Scott was scarcely generous when he observed that the narrative gives no 'new or particular information upon the subjects of the Great Civil War'. If the manuscript makes no major contribution the writer at least strays down byways which escaped the notice of better-known authors. Though the broad outlines of history are not affected by Gwyn's narrative, it serves to fill in numerous gaps. So little is known, for example, about the siege of Faringdon Castle that Gwyn's experiences have their value. The *Memoirs* were written by a veteran who had rendered 'more than six times seven years' service to my king'. Yet he writes with the zest and freshness of a young man. Wounds and imprisonment had not broken his spirit nor hardship disillusioned him.

Gwyn's effort to reduce his narrative to some sort of order is more commendable than effective. (It should be recollected that he was probably bi-lingual in English and Welsh.) He is full of good intentions when he sets out. Though he never intended the manuscript for publication, he divides his work into 'chapters' in a most professional manner, although one 'chapter' contains only four lines and another five and a half. He dispenses with notes, ignores sequence, and jots down incidents as they come to mind. The *Memoirs* are primarily and peculiarly a personal affair. What happens to the army is incidental; what matters is what affects John Gwyn. When, at the First Battle of Newbury, he evades Roundhead broadswords by vaulting a hedge, he dwells more on his escape than on the issue of the conflict.

From random allusions it is possible to form some conception of Gwyn's tribulations during the tedious years of service. In his letter to Sir John Salusbury (son of his first commanding officer) he refers to 'those marks of honour I have got with bloud and wounds and broaken bones'.

The Civil War in England is but part of the story. When he escaped from Scotland after Montrose's betrayal, Gwyn reached Holland, where, on Amsterdam's iron bridge, he 'sunk down dead with mere hunger; and had it not been for the great charity of strangers that revived me, I had gone (for aught I know,) the way of all flesh'. In Flanders he, with Colonel Careless and others, had for their Christmas dinner 'a well-grown young fat dog'. Several times he suffered imprisonment, and on one occasion he escaped death only through the kindness of his jailer.

The *Memoirs* fall into four parts: the war in England; adventures in Scotland and Holland; service under the Duke of York in the

Spanish army in the Netherlands; and a miscellany in which items
which have been overlooked are added. Of these the adventures in
Scotland and the Spanish Netherlands are probably the most important contributions. But with such a haphazard narrative blank
periods are inevitable.

Though Gwyn missed Edgehill he was in time for Brentford a
few weeks later, and from then on he knew no respite. His experiences in the first Civil War are not hard to follow, because it is
possible to trace the movements of his regiment—or rather his first
regiment, for he served in several.

When Gwyn joined the Royal army on Hounslow Heath on the
morning of 12 November, the regiment in which he enlisted was that
led by Sir Thomas Salusbury, Bart, of Lleweni, the paramount house
of Denbighshire. Originally 1,200 strong, it would have been the
King's most powerful infantry regiment at that time. Promoted
ensign on the field, Gwyn accompanied the regiment to Reading and
helped to defend the town; saw the governor, Sir Arthur Aston,
struck on the head by a falling tile; and resented the capitulation by
the deputy-governor, Colonel Richard Feilding. Gwyn's regiment
was at the capture of Bristol, though he does not say so, and from
thence he passed on to the siege of Gloucester. Again, he forgets the
siege in commenting on the appalling weather. It was probably during
the siege of Gloucester that Gwyn saw an arrow strike between the
feet of Sir Jacob Astley; probably, Sir Walter Scott comments, the
last recorded use of arrows in warfare in this country. Gwyn (his
memory is at fault) places the occurrence at Devizes, but Astley was
not there during the siege.

Gwyn was at both Battles of Newbury; and even refers to a
'third' (see p. 62). This was no engagement, but a successful operation by the King and Rupert, who carried off the guns which had
been left under the protection of Donnington Castle after the Second
Battle of Newbury.

On the return from the triumph at Lostwithiel the Royal army
passed through Devizes and the regiment (now commanded by
Colonel (Sir) Charles Lloyd), was left there as garrison. Here they
remained until 23 September 1645, when they surrendered to Cromwell. Officers were separated from their men (some sixty of whom,
according to Symonds, went on to resume the struggle at Bridgnorth) and Gwyn made his way on to Faringdon Castle. He took
service under the Governor, Sir William Courtney, who was so

pleased with his conduct that he made him a company commander (see Part IV). Here he had his leg injured by a stone. It was 'thrice broak afterwards, and never set right'.

It is Gwyn's trivialities which give his *Memoirs* their human appeal. Where great events are concerned he is disappointing. He witnessed many engagements, but only in his account of the Second Battle of Newbury does he make one aware of battle smoke and the clash of arms.

Though he served under Charles I, the Earl of Holland and the Marquis of Montrose, he does not see fit to mention that they were all executed. The Scottish invasion of 1648 is ignored, nor does he allude to the Battle of Preston. Had he done so one might have gained some clue as to the date of a mysterious journey he made to Newcastle. There is no reference to the King's presence there: Gwyn's concern is with his encounter with an intolerant Puritan mayor who turned him out of town. He fared no better in Scotland, for a pass for Holland he wanted was refused him by General David Leslie. Hungry and destitute he had to tramp back to England, forced at times to find a cold couch in a church porch. Whether this occurred in 1646 when Charles was prisoner, or two years later, is difficult to determine. Gwyn's only explanation is that he went 'to see what the Scots would do'.

After the second Civil War broke out in 1648, great events such as the sieges of Colchester and Pembroke, and the Preston battle, are described by other writers to the comparative exclusion of lesser episodes. The revolt at Kingston (which cost the Earl of Holland his head) has been accorded little attention; therefore Gwyn's personal experiences on that unhappy occasion are of considerable interest.

A stormy voyage landed Gwyn in Holland, and in 1649 he was one of the advance-guard under the Earl of Kinnoul, sent ahead of Montrose on the Marquis's fatal venture.

Gwyn visited Scotland a third time (1653), on this occasion to serve under the Earl of Glencairn (transformed by his spelling into 'Clinkern'). From the time he returned to Holland in 1654 until 1657 nothing is known of his movements. He unexpectedly reappears in Flanders, serving under the Duke of York in the Spanish army. He is now a lieutenant in the Royal Regiment of Guards. Although captured in the famous Battle of the Dunes (1658), his eyewitness account is disappointingly curtailed. What is of exceptional interest is the subsequent picture of the sufferings of Gwyn and numerous other

Royalists, many of whom were commissioned officers willing to serve in the ranks to avert starvation.

Because of Gwyn's indifference to the sequence of events, it has been occasionally necessary to rearrange sections or to remove and re-insert passages. These alterations are indicated. Scott's notes are included where relevant marked [*W.S.*]; Gwyn's original notes are marked [*J.G.*]. In certain instances it has been desirable to append fresh notes in the light of new information.

The series of prefatory letters which open the *Memoirs* have been omitted except for the first. See Appendix I, p. 103, for that part of them which contains autobiographical material. In an attempt to link together Gwyn's irregular entries, concise editorial comments are used to introduce his chapters. These have been kept to a minimum so that Gwyn may tell his tale in his own fashion. The gallant captain plunges into his narrative with all the Celtic impetuosity he displayed in rushing the Brentford barricades.

The Military Memoirs of John Gwyn

To his Majesty King Charles II

Sir,

Your Majesty is my best witness to satisfy yourself that I have served you immutably, from youth to old age; nor could any other kind of encouragement on earth gain me from my loyal devotion and service to your Majesty, whilst I had a being in what condition soever; neither would I be so great a criminal, and so insignificant, as some unjustly have rendered me unto your Majesty, for my life. Therefore, and in regard of his Grace the Duke of Monmouth's late commands, that whosoever rides in the Royal troop of Guards, must give an account how long, and in what capacity, he had served the King, and whether gentleman or mechanic; I prepared this small manuscript, of my own poor method and writing, most humbly to present unto your Majesty, a real testimony of those several countries where I have faithfully spent my prime of years in your service, and likewise my observation (as most to the purpose in my best sense,) of all the field-fights and garrisons I have been in, and against, in your Majesty's service. And withal, not one of those many brave fellows who had the honour to carry pikes and muskets when your Majesty, in your junior years, was pleased to exercise us at Richmond and Windsor, nor one from that great nursery of prime men at Court, then about the Royal Family, can own to have gone more steps, and through more hazards, to accomplish his loyal duty, than has,

Your Majesty's most
Humble, faithful,
Poor subject and soldier,
JOHN GWYN.

I

After Edgehill King Charles advanced to Oxford, which he reached on 29 October. Parliament made overtures in the hope of reaching a peaceful compromise, but the King resolved to march on London. The Parliamentarians established a forward post at Brentford, then a small isolated town. Its defence was entrusted to three regiments—the redcoats of Denzil Holles (one of the 'Five Members'), Lord Brooke's purple coats and the renowned John Hampden's greencoats. Their advanced post was along the Isleworth Road, in the house of Sir Richard Wynn, M.P. for Liverpool. Rupert's men crossed Hounslow Heath under cover of darkness. Emerging from the morning mists of 12 November they captured Wynn's house and pushed on to Brentford, but were checked at the barricades which were reinforced by artillery. Gwyn found himself in Sir Thomas Salusbury's regiment of foot which broke through the barriers. Rupert's cavalry charged, and Brentford was in Royalist hands. The victors took 500 prisoners, fifteen guns and eleven colours. Rupert sent Colonel Thomas Blagge to capture Ham House and from this position Royalist guns opened fire on ammunition barges which the Parliamentarians were passing down the Thames. The Royal army's advance was checked by the Parliamentary Captain-General, the third Earl of Essex, at Turnham Green and they retired to winter quarters.

How the King, with his army at Brainford [Brentford], could not advance any further to the purpose towards London than he did, whatsoever were the reports.

The very first day that five comrades of us repaired from the Court at Richmond to the King's royal army, which we met accidentally that morning upon Hounslow Heath, we had no sooner put ourselves into rank and file, under the command of our worthy old acquaintance, Sir George Bunckley, (then Major to Sir Thomas Salsbury,) but we marched up to the enemy, engaged them by Sir Richard Winn's house, and the Thames side, beat them to retreat into Brainford,—beat them from the one Brainford to the other, and from thence to the open field, with a resolute and expeditious fighting, that [*was*] after once firing suddenly to advance up to push of pikes and the butt-end of muskets, which proved so fatal to Holles his butchers and dyers that day, that abundance of them were killed and taken prisoners, besides those drowned in their attempt to escape by leaping into the river. And at that very time were come a great recruit of men to the enemy, both by land and water, from Windsor and Kingston;

and it happened that Sir Charles Lloyd, or some other engineer, to blow up a barge laden with men and ammunition, which, as the fearful crack it gave, and the sad aspect upon't, struck such a terror into the rest of the recruits, that they all vanished, and we better satisfied with their room than their company. Nor can anything of a soldier or an impartial man say, that we might have advanced any further to the purpose towards London than we did, in regard of the thick enclosures, with strong hedges and ditches, so lined with men as they could well stand one by another; and on the common road and other passes, were planted their artillery, with defensible works about them, that there was no coming at them any nearer, upon so great a disadvantage, to do any more than we did, and withal considering that they were more than double our number; therefore the King withdrew, and marched for Hampton Court, where, for my farther encouragement, I had the colours conferred upon me, to go on as I had begun.[1] I cannot omit observing, that had Essex his right wing of horse, which stood upon more ground than the King had horse to face them, wheeled to the left to join with the foot that came from Windsor and Kingston, and fallen on the King's rear, he might have gone to London *nolens volens*.

Having spent a few days at Oatlands, the King established himself at Oxford, which he proceeded to protect by a ring of fortified towns: Banbury, Brill, Wallingford, Abingdon, Faringdon, Burford and (in particular) Reading, which commanded the main route from London to Oxford. Charles visited Reading and placed it in the care of Sir Arthur Aston, giving him a garrison of 3,000 foot and 300 horse. Aston fortified the town with a ditch and high rampart, strengthened by gun-mounts. Several forts protected the outlying high ground. Beyond the top of Castle Hill was a post called the Forlorn Hope which controlled the road to Newbury, and at the top of the hill itself was a fort which guarded the south-west corner of the defences.[2] In addition to the stout walls of its abbey, Reading was protected by the Thames and the Kennet. A short distance away the Thames was crossed by Caversham Bridge, a key position. The garrison included Salusbury's regiment, in which Gwyn served. By 16 April 1643 the Parliamentary army commanded by

[1] This means that Gwyn received a commission as ensign in Salusbury's regiment, no doubt to replace some casualty. He refers later to his carrying the colours at the First Battle of Newbury. At this period each company had its own colours.

[2] Michael Hinton, *A History of Reading*, p. 104 (and map).

*Essex was in a position to lay siege to Reading. Lichfield fell to Rupert on
21 April, while Maurice was at Evesham. Charles hurriedly recalled his
nephews to assist him to relieve the besieged town. The Royalists were
checked at Caversham Fight (25 April) and the King withdrew, leaving his
task unfulfilled. With Aston incapacitated, the deputy-governor, Colonel
Richard Feilding, entered into negotiations with Essex and surrendered the
town. The Parliamentarians broke faith and plundered the captured soldiers.
Feilding was court-martialled and condemned to death, but pardoned. Gwyn
does not hesitate to suggest treachery—a view which was widely held, the
more so because Feilding's brother Basil, now Earl of Denbigh, was a
Parliamentary commander. Whatever Richard Feilding's motive was, he
made every effort to atone.*

*How Sir Arthur Ashton, Governor of Reading, came to be speechless
towards the latter part of the siege, and what ensued upon it.*

From Hampton-Court, his Majesty marched for Reading, fortified it,
made it a garrison, and Sir Arthur Ashton governor, who, upon
receipt of a letter upon the Castle-hill guard, and looking about
him, said, 'Here are none but I may safely communicate the contents
of my letter unto;' then arose from his chair, broke up his letter, and
went out of door to peruse it, when there was no necessity, as want
of light or anything else; but, as his hasty fate would have it, for he
had scarce a minute's time to look it over, but a cannon-shot came
through the guard-house, and drives the tiles about, that one fell upon
his head and sunk him almost to the ground before Colonel [*Henry*]
Lunsford and another officer caught him by both arms,[1] held him up,
brought him into the guard-house, put him into his chair, then presently he laid his hand on his head, under his cap, and faintly said,
'My head's whole, I thank God;' and spoke no more there at that
time, but immediately was carried away to his house in the town,
where, during the rest of the siege, he was speechless;[2] and a considerable time after the garrison was surrendered; then they broke
their conditions with us, and plundered us. Then Colonel Fielding,

[1] As Doctor Jones pressed to come near the governor, a tile fell upon his head, broke it,
and [*it*] bled freely. [*J.G.*]

[2] Clarendon suggests that Ashton was silent out of policy, not choosing to give command
in the state in which he found himself, or not liking the situation of the besieged: at
least, adds the noble historian, 'when he came to Oxford, he could speak as reasonably
of any matter as ever I knew him before or afterwards'. [*W.S.*]

deputy-governor, commanded in chief, who was accused for betraying of the garrison, and condemned to dye at Oxford [4 *May*].

How Reading was betrayed by Fielding

When Colonel Fielding treated with the enemy for the surrender of the garrison, when there was neither want of men, provision, arms, or ammunition, there was sent Captain Whitehead, our scoutmaster-general, and with him went three more commission-officers, for Oxford, to acquaint the King with it.[1] His Majesty was surprised when he heard of it, knowing this frontier garrison to be of a grand consequence, and to have in it as many brave old commanders as was thought to be in all the army besides, sent his positive and strict orders to the governor, and the rest of the officers, that they should take no further notice of whatsoever conference past between them and the enemy, relating to the garrison, but that they should be in readiness to stand in their own defence, if occasion should require, and upon such a day, (naming it, and, as near as he could compute it, the hour of two in the afternoon,) he would come with his army to the relief of us. To second and confirm this his resolution, he was pleased to send a packet by one that swam the river to bring it to the [*deputy*] governor, who so much slighted it, as not to give the least obedience to it at either times; nor when the King came punctually the day prefixt, with his army, to the relief of us, (and some hours sooner than was mentioned, for the King had engaged the enemy by nine or ten of the clock in the morning at Causam Bridge,) yet Fielding was no more concerned at it than if he had been but a neuter to look on and see them fight; and although they broke their truce with us on the other side of the town, in shooting thrice at our royal sconce with their great guns, yet he would not stir, nor consent to make any opposition against them; which is a sufficient demonstration that he designed to render up the garrison quietly to the enemy, as I heard some years after in the remote island of Shetland, upon a discourse with one Harvey, a captain in Sir William Johnson's regiment, under Marquis Montrose, who told me, that at the siege of Reading he was a lieutenant in Essex his life guards, and had the guard upon his tent two several nights, when he saw Fielding go into it to him; and he assured me, that there was nothing more sure than that the garrison was betrayed.

[1] Clarendon says there were but forty barrels of powder in the town. [*W.S.*]

That of Harvey's relation, I presume, was over and above what was in the charge objected against Fielding, when he was condemned to dye, (though afterwards pardoned,) nor would I instance it, but for the inclination I have to render the great probability, that when there was as much corruption in the army as in the garrison, in them, (whatsoever they were that dissuaded the King from his own better judgment and conduct, for he was for coming to the relief of the garrison, though Essex's army was 18,000 strong,) and engage the enemy the same side the river they were on, and take the conveniency of his own time, which would have been a whole night's march; and the next day, possibly, might have been so near as to interpose between several of their troops and drawing up into any great body, being they were quartered far distant one from another; and, as it may well be supposed, their artillery signified but little, for they could not be hurried over hedges and ditches so fast as to any purpose; and then they must have wanted seven or eight thousand of their foot, which was to man their works and line that was of so large a circumference to keep us in play within: and by that and the like means, it would have been very hopeful for the King to succeed against them, and by it preventing the unhappy event that followed by so much ignorance, if not altogether corruption; for they brought the King to engage the enemy, and put the broad deep river of Thames between them, and so to confine his army of horse, foot and artillery, to march over a narrow straight pass, (not much bigger than a sally-port,) of an old wooden bridge, which was within cannon-shot of the enemy's works, and over which there could not march above five, or six at the most, in a breast, and would have taken the remainder of this day to do it; and then they must have drawn the van of their army close to the enemy's works, and the rear upon the brink of the river bank, and yet not have ground enough to draw up an army, if it had been so done as it was not, for the enemy raised a breast-work and a battery against the bridge-end, and the commanded party, or forlorn-hope of the King's army, desperately attempted to force over the bridge against the cannon's mouth, and great bodies of small-shot, which cut them off as fast as they came.

The King was highly troubled at it, and to find that he was over-persuaded to come the wrong way of doing any good, drew off and marched away, with the loss of two or three hundred men, rather than throw away any more of his army upon impossibilities.

And it was much that Essex had not shown more of his military art (if he had it) and let the King's army march over the bridge, and draw up in bodies or into what number he pleased; for they must have been at his devotion, since he might have planted his artillery upon a line, and made quick work with them that had no work, nor no kind of defence for themselves than to expose their naked bodies against a whole train of artillery, and an army of small shot, for they could bring their armies of horse and foot in the rear of their artillery, and face the town at once, for any danger in their flanks or rear, which was as much advantage to them as they could well propose to themselves to have, if they understood it. Much more may be spoke to this; but, in fine, was ever known so gross and shameful an undertaking, under the notion of conduct, as to bring an army to the relief of a place when it lay in the power of one of the enemy to baffle that army; for one man might have cut down an arch of the bridge or unplank it, and so make it inaccessible, before the King with his army could come near it: and which way, then, could he come over with it, had it been ever so advantageous to him, as it was apparently destructive?

The capture of Bristol on 26 July 1643 is overlooked by Gwyn, though he was probably there, for his regiment, now Colonel Lloyd's, participated in the assault. The Royal army passed on to invest Gloucester, where Gwyn was certainly present. Hampered by bad weather, the siege proceeded slowly and Parliament, concerned for the city's safety, dispatched the Earl of Essex with 15,000 men to its relief. Rain had flooded Rupert's mines and with the approach of Essex the siege was abandoned. The King withdrew on 5 September. Charles attempted to get between Essex and London and a race between the two armies ensued. Gwyn comments feelingly about the soaking weather but throws little light on the siege.

How we failed, (as it was then generally reported,) in the taking of Gloucester, which was of so grand consequence.

I was at the siege of Gloucester, where then it was reported, that had there been as much care taken in making one mine ready[1] as was in

---

[1] We learn, from a tract drawn up by Massey the governor, upon the military government of Gloucester during the siege, that the royalists sunk a mine opposite to the east gate of the town, from which they were driven by a desperate sally: also that they renewed their efforts, and notwithstanding the springs, ran a new mine under the moat; while the garrison, by counter-mining, endeavoured to let down the water upon them, or to get at and steal away the powder from the chamber of their mine. [*W.S.*]

making of the other two which stayed for it, probably we had carried the town, and consequently put a period to a great deal of farther trouble; and had not Essex come that very day he did to the relief of it, the land-flood, which, by a great glut of rain fell that night, had made all our labour in vain, and we forced to remove the next day.

[*The following incident appears to belong to this period.*] I having guard by the river side, and standing by Sir Jacob Ashley, a bearded arrow stuck into the ground between his legs. He plucked it out with both hands, and said, 'You rogues, you missed your aim.'[1]

The two armies now raced for position. Two days' rest was all that Essex allowed his foot-weary soldiers. Gwyn's observations indicate that the Royal army was in no better plight. It had, however, a slight start and reached Newbury ahead of the Parliamentarians. Essex on 15 September captured Cirencester and in the town took most of the two regiments of Sir Nicholas Crispe and Colonel Richard Spencer, the latter from Kent, the former officered by Londoners. Essex also secured much-needed provisions. On 20 September the First Battle of Newbury was fought. Both armies were approximately equal in size, but the Cavaliers were superior in cavalry. A prolonged and confused conflict continued until nightfall, by which time the Royal army was short of powder. While weary troops rested the King withdrew in the darkness, leaving Essex free to return to London while the Royal forces made for Oxford.

First engagement at Newberry. Newberry Fight was not quite ended, until, in the pursuit of Essex, we took Reading.

And when we drew off, it proved to be a most miserable tempestuous, rainy weather, that few or none could take little or no rest on the hills where they were; and the unceasing winds next morning soon dried up our through-wet clothes we lay pickled in all night, (as a convenient washing of us at our coming from the trenches;) and we made such haste in pursuit of Essex's army, that there was an account given of fifteen hundred foot quite tired and spent, not possible to come up to their colours before we engaged the enemy; and a night

[1] This is perhaps the last mention of the use of bow and arrow in England in actual battle. In Montrose's wars, many of the remote Highlanders continued to act as archers; but in England, the once formidable long bow had, in the middle of the seventeenth century, fallen into almost total desuetude. [*W.S.*]

or two before [*15 September*], we lost two regiments of horse, (Kentish men, and new raised regiments,) which were surprised and taken prisoners in their quarters; and what was worse, in most men's opinion, we were like to drop down every step we made with want of sleep; yet, notwithstanding, we marched on still, until the evening we overtook the enemy's army at Newberry town's end; then our quarter-masters, with their party, beat their quarter-masters and their parties of horse out of the town, and very early in the morning gave them battle.

How, upon some engagements, that exercise which your Majesty, in your junior years, was often pleased to command me to practice before you, hath under God, preserved me when there was no other visible help.

At Newberry first fight, when we beat the enemy upon all disadvantage, from the town's end to the top of the hill by the heath, a wing of Essex his horse moving gently towards us,[1] made us leave our execution upon the enemy, and retreat into the next field, where were several gaps to get to it, but not direct in my way; yet, with the colours in my hand, I jumped over hedge and ditch,[2] or I had died by multitude of hands. We kept this field until midnight, and until some intelligence came that Essex was marching away with a great part of his army, and that he had buried a great many of his great guns by two of the clock in the afternoon. Near unto this field, upon the heath, lay a whole file of men, six deep, with their heads all struck off with one cannon shot of ours. We pursued Essex in his retreat, took Reading without opposition, made it a garrison, and Sir Jacob Ashley governor.

The second of the next two sections presents a complicated problem. It opens with Cropredy Bridge (29 June 1644) and then deals with the Second Battle of Newbury (27 October). Between the first and second sentences Gwyn marches to Cornwall to witness the surrender of Essex's infantry at Lost-withiel (2 September). In his last sentence he returns to Cropredy Bridge again. As if this were not sufficiently bewildering, his account of saving Cawfield's life really belongs to Cropredy Bridge and not to Second Newbury. The name of Cornet Cawfield, brother to the Lord Cawfield, occurs

---

[1] The right wing of the Parliamentarian horse under Colonel Sir Philip Stapleton.

[2] Possibly by pole-vaulting.

*among the prisoners taken from Waller's army at Cropredy Bridge (Mer-
curius Aulicus, 1644 p.1056). This section is left undisturbed, as to rearrange
it would make confusion worse confounded. In fairness to Gwyn it should
be remembered that he wrote nearly forty years after the events. Scott's note
seems of unusual interest.*

*In the spring of 1644 Reading was abandoned, and the armies of
Waller and Essex menaced the King's position at Oxford. Charles slipped
out of the city and marched to Worcester, which he reached on 6 June, but,
fearing he might be trapped between two armies, he did not remain. Essex
and Waller threw away their opportunity by deciding to part company. The
outcome was Waller's defeat by the King at Cropredy Bridge.*

*How twenty-seven officers and reformadoes went designedly ten miles
upon the downs, to charge the rear-guard of an army, singing[1] and
fighting.*

When [*on 3 June 1644*] the King marched with his army from Oxford
to Killington [*Kidlington*] Green, to attend Essex and Waller's motion,
it appeared their design was to go to the west, as they did, though they
divided their armies and marched several ways, as though it would
be most convenient for their better accommodation, being asunder;
yet still they followed one another westward, and we followed after
them, and beat them one after another, which would have been a
harder task for us to do had they kept together, as it was admired
they did not. Two accidents occurred at this time to us. A party of
the enemy's horse marched amongst us, as some of our own men, call
Mr Sackfield [*Edward Sackville*] out of his quarters, mount him and
steal him away.[2] Also a soldier's bandolier, who guarded the colours,
took fire, and went off in a heat, which made an incredible confusion
amongst us.

*How we overtook Waller's army, which we engaged and beat
[29 June 1644].*

At Crobedery Bridge, and thereabouts, we overtook Waller's army,
which we engaged and beat, and took [*James*] Wemes, general of

---

[1] Gwyn forgets to describe the incident. See p. 64.

[2] Gwyn's recollection is at fault here. It was on 18 April 1646 that Mr Sackville, second
son to the Earl of Dorset, was killed near Witham by seven foot soldiers from Abingdon
(*Dugdale's Diary*, p. 85).

their artillery, prisoner;[1] and withal took his leather guns,[2] which proved very serviceable to the King. The second Newberry fight at Dolman's House [i.e. *Shaw House*], and, my going a volunteer with my worthy friend Major Richard Lloyd, who was upon a commanded party, as worth to my Lord Caulfield his life that day, for just as he came out of the mill, stripped and wounded, a lusty soldier was fetching of a desperate blow with the butt-end of his musket, to make an end of him, which of a sudden I prevented, and made him prisoner upon the top of the hill by the windmill. He was examined before the King, and declared he was Lord Caulfield's son, of Ireland, and a cornet in the Parliament service: and Wemes was severely rebuked by his Majesty for deserting his service. and to come in arms against him.

Before dealing with the Second Battle of Newbury, which was one of the turning-points of the war, Gwyn alludes briefly to his experience at Lostwithiel. The fight against odds at Second Newbury evidently made a profound impression on Gwyn, who devotes several disconnected chapters to his recollections. These have been rearranged in what appears to be the right sequence. Though the Parliamentary cavalry under Balfour broke out and escaped from the Lostwithiel calamity, the entire Parliamentary foot under the redoubtable Skippon were compelled to lay down their arms. Essex left his army to its fate and escaped by ship. The weary Royalist army set out to trudge back to Oxford. The Parliament, recovering from the shock, rallied three armies to block the path of the King, whom they imagined to be heading for London. The King's situation looked hopeless, but by sheer courage the Royalists fought three armies to a standstill. Then in the darkness they

---

[1] Wemyss had been created by Charles master-gunner of England, with a pension of £300 a year, which, as he was a Scotchman, gave some distaste to the English. Nevertheless he embraced the cause of the Parliament very keenly, and became master of Essex's ordnance. He seems to have been an engineer of some invention and ingenuity, supposing him to have been the same Colonel James Wemyss, to whom, in 1661, the Scottish Parliament granted a monopoly of 'several inventions of light ordnance, throwing from ane quarter of ane pund bullet to ane demi-cannon that carries ane threttie-twa pund shot, and other engines of war, as mortar-pieces, pillards, sufficient experience whereof was seen at Gogar fight, Lerber Bridge, and elsewhere'; allowing to him, as inventor, the exclusive sale thereof to subjects and strangers for the space of 'three nineteen years'. [*W.S.*]

[2] These small brass and leather guns, seven in number, were mounted in barricadoes of wood, each of which stood on wheels, and thus formed a species of moving battery [*W.S.*]

effected a stealthy withdrawal and marched away to safety, leaving their artillery under the works of Donnington Castle. That Charles should have been brought to battle in such a situation seemed to Gwyn to reflect on the capacity of the King's generals.

How the King's impaired army, after beating two several armies one after another, after exceedingly hard marches; and after his Majesty had commanded fifteen hundred horse[1] to the relief of Banbury, was engaged by three fresh armies and engaged in his royal person [27 October 1644].

Having thus cleared the way, we arrived with less trouble into Corn-wall, where likewise we routed Essex, took all his army of infantry prisoners, with arms, ammunition, and artillery, and sent him packing to sea; whereupon it was conceived to be far easier for us to have defeated his forlorn shattered cavalry, being left to shift for them-selves, than it was to defeat them both in their united strength, as we did, or at least to have forced them to embrace such conditions as was by capitulation made in that country by Lord Hopton and [*Sir Thomas*] Fairfax,[2] and then it had been impossible for them (like Hydras) to have so increased into three armies, as they did when they met the King in his return from Cornwall, [*at*] the second Newberry fight. The King in his speech to Reading soldiers, desired that his word of a Prince might be kept inviolably, though they break their conditions, saying, 'What is't but a rebel dare do?'[3]

How a party of three hundred men made a sally upon a regiment of fifteen hundred, and, after a long dispute, beat them clear out of the field.

The day before the second Newberry fight, when the King had made an end of his march, and was encamped about three or four of the clock in the afternoon, within a mile and a half (or thereabouts) of Newberry, news came that Bambury was besieged; whereupon his Majesty was pleased to command the Earl of Northampton to go with

[1] The Earl of Northampton's brigade, really about 800 strong, not 1,500.

[2] The Treaty of Truro, 1646, by which Hopton disbanded his army.

[3] The author alludes to the capture of Reading, which was ill observed by the Round-heads. But, notwithstanding the expressions in the text, this breach of the treaty was made frequently a plea for retaliation when the Royalists found an opportunity; And this led on each side to repeated breaches of articles of surrender or treaty. [*W.S.*]

his brigade of fifteen hundred horse to the relief of it; when, in the meantime, the King, for his own part, I dare swear, knew not in the least, nor did not in the least suspect, that on the other side of the town were three armies, drawn up upon the most advantageous ground they could pitch and choose, to fight him; had his Majesty received but the least hint of this, certainly he would not have so much weakened his impaired harassed army, after the defeating of two armies, soon one after another, and after the loss of so many men killed and wounded, as to part with fifteen hundred of his best horse, when the very next day he was perforce to fight the three armies which waylaid him, and withal was conducted into a trap, which the enemy had laid to do it. Howsoever it came about, for when the King marched with his army fair and orderly through the town, into the spacious Spinham Lands [*Speenhamland*] there, he drew up, as near as he possibly could be, in the centre of his enemies; for right before him were posted Essex and Waller's armies, drawn up in the enclosures, and in ambushes of hedges and ditches, and fronted with cannon to maintain that pass. On his right wing was Manchester's army of seven thousand, (some of themselves have declared that they were ten thousand,) to wheel and fall on his rear. On his left wing was the deep river [*Kennet*], as considerable as another army, to enclose and hem him in amongst them as they did. His Majesty, being thus pinfolded with walls of armed men, every way ready to execute their fury upon him when he did but stir, advanced, with the major part of his army, against the cannon's mouth, to get to charge the two armies, which were so strongly linked together against him; and at their encounter, there was very hot fiery dispute, that the thundering peals and volleys of great and small guns, were sufficient sign for Manchester and Cromwell to fall on the King's rear with their army of seven thousand, as they did very boldly, desperately fought it, and were most wonderfully paid off, by fourteen hundred commanded men[1] out of his Majesty's army, as before mentioned. All this while the King was laying on with all eagerness imaginable, to beat through the two armies, which were so wickedly stubborn and obstinate, that they rather made to a head, and forst him back further and further into Spinham Lands, that both the enemy's armies were in the open field at close fight with the King and his army, and put them so hard to it, that his Majesty was engaged in his royal person, General

[1] Colonel George Lisle's tertia.

Ruthin [*Ruthven Lord Forth*] wounded fighting by his side, and several persons of quality killed by them.[1] This height of extremity the King was in, did so exasperate the great spirit of his approved brave cavaliers, that they fell on with invincible courage, and pouthered [*sic*] them back into their enclosures of hedges and ditches. Then the night drew on, and parted us with a seeming joint consent on both sides, for we marched away with our army all night by them, and they did not in the least disturb us, nor we gave them no occasion in the least for it; and so we came off to admiration. The next morning we marched for Oxford, not without some skirmishing in the rear. If Manchester had any good inclinations towards the King, why did he accept of Cromwell for his Lieutenant-general, who was so inveterate an enemy to the King and his government?

How Manchester, with his army of seven thousand horse and foot (when Cromwell was his Lieutenant-General,) were most shamefully beaten out of the field by a party of fourteen hundred commanded men out of the King's army.

The second Newberry fight, we drew up upon the same ground which the enemy fought us upon the first battle.[2] After our long march from Cornwall, and great want of intelligence, we were exposed unavoidably to fight three fresh armies, which waylaid the King to oppose his march; whereupon a most remarkable piece of service was done by the great contrivance of Major-General Lord Ashley [*Astley*] and great performance of eight hundred foot, commanded by Colonel [*Anthony*] Thelwall; four hundred foot commanded by [*Lt-Col.*] Sir Richard Page, at Dolman's House; two hundred horse commanded by Sir George Lysle, in the interval between Dolman's House and the field Thelwall was in. These fourteen hundred thus posted, beat off twice Manchester's army of seven thousand horse and foot; and at their third and last onset, beat them clear out of the field, and stripped abundance of them. Some few hours after, my Lord Ashley marched away with us by moonshine,

---

[1] The enemy carried the village of Speen at the first onset; and their right wing of horse advanced with such fury as to disorder those of the King. Even the presence of Charles himself could not restrain his cavalry from giving ground; and his own person had been in great danger, but for a gallant and desperate charge made by the Queen's regiment of horse, under command of Sir John Cansfield. [*W.S.*]

[2] The positions were not identical. The first battle was south of the River Kennet.

and of necessity, through a narrow filthy pass of puddle and mire, just by the hedge-side that parted us and the two armies, Essex and Waller's, who were as quiet as if they had taken the same opportunity of drawing off too, and doubtless would have been forced to it, had not the King commanded fifteen hundred prime horse to the relief of Bambury, when it was too late to call them back to our assistance, and for us to avoid fighting, being so strangely surprised as we were: but, I presume, that a forced putt [*thrust*] was never better managed, nor came off with more honour, as to beat one army away, the other two out of the way, and so cleared our way, lodged our artillery at Denington Castle,[1] and marched for Oxford.

Retreat after the second fight of Newbery, and reflections thereon.

And the messenger that came to the King by Newbery, and brought him intelligence that Bambury was besieged, might as well at the same instant tell him, that on the other side of the town were three armies [that] waylaid him; then, perhaps, he had thought fit to keep on the same side of the town he was on, and plant some of his great guns against the town's end and the river side, and let the enemy that had pursued him fall on upon his cannon's mouth (if they liked it) rather than do as he did, fall upon theirs; and if the King did approve of so doing, then he could easily march away that night, and send to his army at Oxford, and to the Earl of Northampton, to come and meet him where he thought convenient. All that the enemy could do that night, was to disperse orders for the three armies to make ready for a march the next morning, which had been a great trouble to decamp, bring off their carriages, draw up and march through the narrow town, and then draw up on the other side of it, which would take up most part of the day, and give the King almost a day and a night's march before them, to meet his other army: and, if the enemy durst hasard one of their armies to interpose (if they could) between the King's army from Oxford, and meeting with him, then he could better fight with two armies than with three, and upon his own choice of ground, and the assistance of the brave Earl of Northampton, with his brigade of fifteen hundred brave horse: and questionless the army from Oxford had rather engage one of the enemy's armies, than keep off and let them all three at once fall upon the King, as they

1 Donnington Castle. The royal garrison was under Sir John Boyes who commanded 200 foot and twenty-five horse.

did at this second Newbery fight, by the strange conduct of them who marched away with the King and his army from Cornwall, as far as to Newbery; as if he had been blind and deaf that he could neither see nor hear of an enemy until he could not march a field further, but must stumble upon them for any notice he had of them.

The author's impartiality shewn in his defence of Manchester and Cromwell.[1]

The Parliament needed not to question Manchester or Cromwell for that day's work, though it rendered a foul suspicion in their conduct, to be so shamefully beaten: but it clearly appeared they were outdone in soldiership and policy; for when they, with their army, first marched over the ground, and had the full survey of it, they did not so well apprehend the advantage that was to be made of it, as did our major-general, Lord Ashley, who, from his great experience and quick apprehension, had no sooner cast his eye upon't, but he manned those places, and presently commands a great body of horse to stand as a blind between us and the enemy, and picqueer [*skirmish*] with them. In the meantime, Colonel Thelwell was making up of the gaps in the quickset-hedge, which he was to maintaine, and making of the ditch under it deeper and wider; Sir George Lysle and Sir Richard Page were fixing of themselves, as well as they could, at their posts. Then orders were given to Thelwell not to give fire upon the enemy until they came within a pike's length of him. Sir Richard Page needed no such orders, for they came near to him as they moved by: nor could they come to charge Sir George Lysle but through the enemy's fire, for Sir Richard Page with his leather guns, loaden with key-shot [*caseshot?*], and his four hundred musketeers in the dry moat, played between the pailes [*palings*] upon the flanks of them; and Thelwell, with his body of musketeers, likewise played through the quickset-hedge in their teeths, that made a heavy slaughter among them, maimed and so disabled them, that they came in disorder to charge Sir George Lysle, which made him the better able to defend himself against so powerful an opposition: and it is observable, that sometimes great commanders have miscarried, in too much slighting of an enemy, and trusting to their own strength: and it is very like those two commanders were under the same mistake, deceived as

[1] The title is ironical. The author only defends them against the charge of being false to what he considered as their disloyal cause. [*W.S.*]

presuming too much in their exceeding number of men, which, in all probability, might fairly promise them victory, having on their side more than six to one the odds of it; and withal knew, that at the same instant the King was hotly engaged in close fight with the other two armies, which were so severe upon him, that he was forced to send for my Lord Hopton to come to his assistance, who was a reserve to Sir George Lysle; and he could as ill spare him at that time, that it was thought impossible for him to be without him or some other reserve: but that Sir George did wonders to maintain his post with that party of his own men, without a reserve, and so bravely encouraged them to stick close to him (the King being engaged in the next field in his royal person,) that he threw off his upper garments to charge in his shirt, whereupon they all unanimously, as one man of one mind, resolved to live and die with him upon the spot, fought it courageously, and came off victoriously; and if Essex and Manchester deserved the name of having any kindness for the King, as it was rumoured amongst us, they could not have a better opportunity to express it than at that time at Newbery; for they were the Parliament's strength and masters, if they pleased to do the King and themselves the right as to own it; nor they never before had so much of clear and undoubted reason to know their own palpable errors, and his goodness and clemency, for there were some thousands of soldiers fought against him that day, who knew very well that the King very lately had given them their lives in Cornwall, when it lay justly in his power to cut them all off, banish them, or imprison them, and did neither, but bid them go home and be honest men: and rather than they would do so, did according to an old proverb,—'Save a thief from the gallows, and he will hang you if he can:' so they doubled and trebled their forces, to come and cut him off, and had sacrificed him that day, to all men's opinion, but that it was more God's will to defend him, than any kindness they showed him.

Further argument on the second Battle of Newbery.

And though the King beat Essex, made him fly for't, took all his army of foot prisoners [at Lostwithiel], and, from his too much tenderness and pity, remitted them; yet there was no reason that any should persuade his Majesty that then he was secure from having any more enemies in England, since there were forces in the north against him,—since Waller, with his beaten army, hastened for London to recruit,—since Manchester and Cromwell were about London, with an army ready,—and since some of the King's great commanders did no better than play booty [*false*], to let Essex his remnant of shattered horse go after his foot, saying, 'Ever make a golden bridge for your enemy'. So when the King could have blocked up all the lane's-end they were to march through with his artillery, face them with his army, and send such conditions as his Majesty should think expedient, which must needs be acceptable, considering his abundant goodness, and their own forlorn desperate condition at that present; they let them go by consent after their foot to recruit, which they did with so much haste and great performance, that before the King, with his army, could march from Cornwall, within a little more than a mile of Newbery, the enemy's armies, all three, were come on the other side of the town, and there stayed, lurking in obscurity, till the King marched into their mouths, for he drew up within their arms of pikes and muskets, that he could not stir neither front, flank, or rear, but upon their fire; and had it not been for his great fighting, and more for the great providence that attended him in that imminent danger, he had not come off so well as he did.

Third engagement at Newbery [*9 November 1644*].

The third Newbery, we went for our artillery, and with a resolution to fight, if we found the enemy to appear so too; for we drew up, and we offered them battle; but they declined it, only skirmished a little insignificantly, and we at leisure marched away with our artillery.

A Parliament officer of my acquaintance, who was then there told me the reason why they would not engage with us, was, because one of their armies was commanded away.

Devizes, an important stopping centre for Royalists journeying between Oxford and the West, played a conspicuous part in Gwyn's early campaigning. It would seem that Sir Charles Lloyd's Regiment (ex-Salusbury's) on the way back from the triumph at Lostwithiel was stationed here as garrison, though it is clear that a commanded party under Major Richard Lloyd took part in the second Battle of Newbury. After Naseby, when the tide of war turned, Devizes was strengthened in anticipation of a siege. Sir Charles Lloyd's experience as an engineer was valuable although he has been criticized for not making a more stubborn defence when attacked by

Cromwell. Devizes Castle surrendered on 23 September and the Regiment was broken up, the soldiers being separated from their officers. Symonds records the arrival of 60 at Bridgnorth. From Gwyn's own account it is apparent that he went on to Faringdon Castle where the governor, Sir William Courtney, recognized the worth of this tried and courageous officer. In Part IV Gwyn records further incidents which occurred before the place was besieged, probably in the spring of 1645.

Gwyn may well have been one of Sir Charles Lloyd's four captains, who fought in the forlorn hope, in the skirmish at Aldbourne early in August 1645. It seems improbable, however, that this was the episode which he describes as the routing of Waller's rearguard at Marlborough town's end.

'*Sir Charles Lloyd, Colonel* [James] *Long* [High Sheriff of Wiltshire], *and Major* [Francis] *Dowet, marched from the Devizes with 100 horse and 20 dragoons, and hearing that 300 of the rebels' horse and 60 dragoons (commanded by one Martin) were refreshing themselves in Auburne* [Aldbourne], *they resolved to fall upon them. For which purpose they disposed themselves into 4 parties, Major Dowet commanded the forlorn hope (the officers were Reformadoes except 4 of Sir Charles Lloyd's captains) who without any alarm fell in among the rebels, and cleared the town; the Major and all other officers did their parts gallantly, and had taken 60 prisoners: but some common soldiers in the Reserve dispersing themselves to plunder among the rebels, gave the rebels time to rally, and fall on with much advantage while the soldiers were thus scattered. Yet after some skirmishing (with loss of 4 men whom they took prisoners) the rebels were all beaten quite out of the town, flying several ways; but execution was not persued, for the prisoners confessed that* [Richard] *Fincher (the rebels' Quartermaster-General) was at hand with 500 fresh horse to relieve them; so as they timely retreated, having 18 long miles home to the Devizes, where they came safe with 17 prisoners, whereof 2 were lieutenants, divers good horses taken, but especially the dragoons exchanged their tired jades for the rebels' best horses.*'[1]

The Author's gallantry at the Devizes [1645?]

When a party of Waller's horse beat up our quarters at the Devizes, and furiously scoured the streets, giving no quarters to any soldiers they met, then I run and leaped across the street of such a sudden by them as to escape both their swords and pistols, when they killed Captain Jones, with others, and shot Ensign Garroway in the neck.

[1] *Mercurius Aulicus*, 12 August 1645.

And to be quit with them, a knot of my own associates, officers and reformadoes, belonging to the garrison, came to pass away an hour or two with me at my quarters, and there contracted to make a party, to go and fall upon Waller's rear-guard at Marlborough town end; and withal strictly resolved, that not a word should be spoken after once their swords were drawn, but all to march on in order, and unanimously to sing a brisk lively tune, (being a great part of their design) and so to fall on singing as they did;[1] beat the enemy, and pursued them through the town at mid-day, and market-day too; which so rejoiced a number of loyal-hearted market-people, that their loud shouts gave an apprehension as if an army had come to second them. This strong alarm did so discompose their whole camp, that this small party had time enough to make good their long retreat, and to bring with them their well deserved prize they so fought bravely for, of prisoners, horse, and arms, without the loss of a man, and but one or two slightly wounded.

How the Devizes was taken, the rather by the absence of those who were obliged to come unto it, and did not.

I was in the garrison of the Devizes, where Fairfax and Cromwell were at a stand whether they had best meddle with us, until they came to understand that the horse in quarters thereabout were not come into it, which upon all occasion were obliged. Then they laid close siege to us. One or two soldiers had run over the works to the enemy, and informed them how all things stood with us, or they had not besieged us. The enemy, with incessant peals of muskets, great guns, and mortar-pieces, played upon us, that it past us all day and night at our line, without the least reserve, that we could do no more, when we might have done better with our respected numbers, we resigned.

Of strange preservations which were vouchsafed to the Author.

At the Devizes, as I sat upon a small seat of sods, with my back to an empty cannon-basket, which lay close to the works'-side, a sergeant that stood by calls me up in all haste, to show me three of the enemy, (officer like,) that came to discover our works. I had no sooner started up, but he clapped down in my place; nor was he no sooner

[1] The twenty-seven mentioned in Gwyn's first heading on p. 54.

sat, but a musket-ball struck through the basket into his head, and he died immediately.

After the surrender of Devizes Gwyn offered his services to the governor of Faringdon Castle, one of the fortified places which formed the outer defences of Oxford. It had acquired some fame as one of the few places which succeeded in repulsing Cromwell. This was in the spring of 1645 (29 April). When summoned to surrender the governor, Lieutenant-Colonel Roger Burges of Sir John Owen's Regiment of Foot, replied: 'You are not now at Bletchingdon.' Cromwell immediately began the assault but was beaten off with loss. Gwyn probably reached Faringdon Castle about the end of September 1645.

Of a sally I made upon a guard of fifty of the enemy, killed, wounded, and took prisoners all but one or two, in less than three minutes' time.

Upon a discourse with [*Colonel*] Sir William Courtney, (then Governor of Farington,) who told me he was really persuaded that I had an antipathy against a runaway cavalier; and that there was fifty or sixty of them kept a guard in the Town Pesthouse, and asked of me if I would take a party and go and correct them, for deserting the King's service to turn rebels, I embraced it, and presently went upon the battery to see what way best I might go to work; and by my observations, I could not apprehend any way possible of doing any good against them, for the Pesthouse was some three hundred paces distant from any part of our works. It had but one door, which was three quarters made up with sods, full of musket loop-holes; they had works and guards on that side of the town, within a quoit's cast of ours, that we could not stir but they must know of it; and then they had a party of horse day and night attending at the main-guard upon all occasions. These objections I would not make, though very excusably I might, to Sir William Courtney, or to any of them, for their advice; but went on my own way, being it was put upon me: and as I concluded with myself that there was one way for it, that I took, hit or miss. And it happened to be as I conjectur'd: for, by a flash of fire which came so low from the house, and the help of a perspective-glass,[1] I made a discovery that the musket loop-holes were but breast-high without, and therefore of consequence, must be so

[1] This must have been one of the first references to its use, especially by a junior officer.

within. Then I went to the Governor, and told him that I was now ready for his commands, and that I would have every musketeer to load his musket with three carbine-balls made into cartridges; and likewise told the soldiers to file and run after me as fast as they could, and round the house, stooping under the musket loop-holes, which we presently commanded from the enemy, and poured in shot so fast, that they immediately cried out for quarters, which they had; and in that short time of action their horse came to their relief, and in a manner charged our horse, which were my reserve, who shrunk a little, that I had been lost, being so far in the rear of the party that was going away with the prisoners, but for twelve or fourteen brave men of my special friends, who were resolved to bring me off, or fall themselves.

[*This must be the occasion on which Mr Juell was killed as Gwyn relates*.] Upon a retreat of a sally from Farrington when one Mr Juell (an accomplished gentleman,) and a corporal of the garrison, failed to jump over a broad deep ditch under the enemy's works, were both killed, I jumped just after them, and quite over, or I might have been anatomized as Mr Jewell was.

An account of one particular action which I performed in every country that I served your Majesty.[1]

To Farrington garrison I came, a stranger amongst those eminent soldiers: three hundred of them made a sally upon a siege of fifteen hundred men; fought them three hours and three quarters exactly by Sir William Courtney's watch; beat them from their works and guards, to retreat into strong houses of the town: then we fetched some of our artillery, forced them thence; and when they rallied, routed them in the open field. For my service amongst them, the Governor was pleased to confer a company upon men, as a reward, and my encouragement.[2]

Another [preservation].

At Farington garrison, as I was coming down stairs, and stooping very low, to look upon an accident which happened to both my legs,

---

[1] This and the following section, originally in Part IV, belong to this period.

[2] Justice (of the Peace) Rosewell, then my lieutenant-colonel, who preserved my life in prison, will confirm this. [J.G.]

a cannon-shot came through the house, and over my head, just that very moment I stooped, and struck into the stairs, between me [and] a gentleman that followed me; and though I saved my head by it, yet I had so severe a blow upon my leg, by a stone which came from the wall that proved very ominous; for where I received the blow, there my leg was thrice broke afterwards, and never set right. The first time it was broke, was the least of two mischiefs that attended me upon a loyal account, which I had rather speak then write, if requisite.

The Author's loyalty at Farington

At the surrender of Farington [*24 June 1646*], (which was the same with Oxford condition), where were two hundred lusty soldiers offered to take their fortune with me wheresoever I went or engaged, which made the enemy tender a field officer's command unto me, if I would bring with me those men, and take up arms with them, to go against the Scots; or if I came alone, I should have a company, being so well known amongst them upon several accounts, and withal urged several arguments to dissuade me from having any thoughts that the Scots army came to do the King any service, whatsoever they pretended; but their invitation upon that account did not at all relish with me, though I had neither lands, goods nor tenements, to relieve myself, nor friends or relations, that I knew where to find or how they stood affected in so long a discontinuance of time: and when I came to London, I was in so many plots and engagements, that at last I was thrown into prison, which had cost me my life, but for my keeper, who, for my life, I was never since able to gratify, nor any other who in those days have highly obliged me: And when, by my keeper's means, I got my liberty, the fourth or fifth day after, I was presented by Sir Thomas Sandys, upon Kingston-Heath, to be the first captain in the Earl of Holland's regiment of guards.[1]

I omitted to insert in any other of my manuscripts, that in prison it was offered unto me, if I would be banished, and swear never to serve the King, perhaps I should have my enlargement; but at my dislike of it upon those terms, I was told in short what I was to expect: then, in case my designs, which before I had time to force my liberty, should fail me, and to satisfy my friends why I had rather die than live and swear never to serve my King, nor any of that royal race; I

[1] The last sentence seems to be out of order, for it refers to 1648. See p. 68.

expressed it as well as I could, in few lines I made in verse upon my inseparable devotion to loyalty I called mistress; with my invective in a short character of Cromwell, and his never-to-be forgotten Long Parliament, who had hanged me for my loyalty, but for my honest keeper.

Upon my inseparable devotion to Loyalty I called Mistress

> I am so fond a lover grown,
> That for my mistress' cause could die;
> Nor would enjoy my love alone,
> But wish her millions more than I.
>
> I am devoted to her hand;
> A willing sacrifice could be,
> If she be pleased but to command,
> To die is easy unto me.

Cromwell's Character

> He's a sort of a devil, whose pride so vast,
> As he were thrown beyond Lucifer's cast,
> With greater curse, that his plagues may excel
> In killing torments, and a blacker hell!

Upon the Long Parliament

> They tire the devil, for they would be worse
> Than he himself, when he received a curse;
> Sure it pained him to hatch so foul a brood,
> Vile, pickled villains, damned through every mood,
> Oh! strange they are not swallowed where they sit,
> 'Tis blasphemy to think what they commit.

The preceding and the following two sections are puzzling particularly on account of the absence of any dates. Early in May 1646 the King escaped from Oxford and gave himself up at Newark to the Scots who removed him to Newcastle to be nearer the Border. Here Charles remained until the Scots went home at the end of January 1647. On the surrender of Faringdon (June 1646) Gwyn was offered (he avers) a commission as major in the Parliamentary army if he would serve with them against the Scots. There seems to be some doubt about this as the Scots at this time were allies of Parliament. Gwyn became involved in 'so many plots and engagements' near London that he was finally flung into prison. The next identifiable reference is to his being given a captain's commission in the Earl of Holland's

Regiment which must be early in 1648.[1] *On 4 July the Earl of Holland, the Earl of Buckingham and the latter's youngest brother, Lord Francis Villiers, left London to appear at Kingston at the head of a group of loyal gentlemen. The Earl failed to rally more than 600 supporters. On 7 July Holland was overtaken and after a skirmish was driven into Kingston. The Cavaliers fought bravely but were overcome. Gwyn seems to have been taken prisoner, and this may be the occasion when his life was saved by his 'honest keeper'.*

There follows Gwyn's appearance before 'Oliver's Lords'. Cromwell, still second-in-command to Fairfax, had no 'Lords' nor could he create them until he was Protector. Gwyn doubtless meant 'judges'. 'Scot', Clerk to the Council (? of State) must be Thomas Scott, M.P. for Aylesbury in the Long Parliament, who was executed as a regicide in 1660. The incident was earlier than 1649 in which year the Council of State appointed Scott 'to manage the intelligence both at home and abroad for the state'. At the fall of the Parliament Scott fled overseas.

It is not easy to position Gwyn's mysterious journey to Newcastle (p. 70): 'to see what the Scots would do'. This is ambiguous. If he went to Newcastle to aid the King (as the town's name implies), the sentence is out of context; if he went, as its position indicates, in 1648, it is amazing that there is no reference to arrangements for the Duke of Hamilton's invasion which was shattered at Preston. The conclusion must be that Gwyn's memory played him false and that he has confused several incidents.

Of some replies I made when examined before the enemy.

When I was brought a prisoner, to be examined before Oliver's Lords at Westminster, [*Thomas*] Scot, clerk to the Council, demands why I writ that the Parliament and the army were such two sore plagues to the kingdom? I told him, because they ruined the King and his friends. The Lords were no sooner gone, but he most inveterately says, 'Sirrah, thou art a villain in thy heart! and, if I live, I will see thee hanged.' But it lay not in his power; for he had not been so soon taken where he was, but for me, tho' others had the repute and reward for it.[2]

Nor had the regiment of Guards in Flanders, for twice or thrice,

---

[1] Confirmed by the entry in *A List of [Indigent] Officers, 1663*.

[2] In April 1660 Scott, having fled in disguise to Flanders, was recognized in Brussels. Eventually he surrendered himself to Sir Henry de Vic, the King's resident. Credit for his capture or surrender was much disputed (*Cal. State Papers, Dom.*, 1670, p. 649). He was brought to England and executed.

continued a regiment there but for my care and management, tho' I am no more the better for't than that I have done others good in it.

Remarks upon the defeat at Kingston.[1]

The people of Kingston understood very well our design; and most of them, being loyally affected, have voluntarily offered to send provision enough into the field for us, and to arm all our unarmed men; and questionless would have assisted us too, had they seen any conduct amongst us: but the general would not accept of any thing from them, but must needs march with us all into the town, which gave the enemy an opportunity to fall in upon our rear-guard, where that truly honourable and brave Lord Francis[2] was killed; and in a few days after, some of the enemy where I had been, acknowledged, that had our rear-guard been completely armed as some had swords and no pistols, others with pistols and no swords, we had beat them; or had they seen but a file of men come to our relief, they had gone; or had we rendezvoused on the heath all night, it had been well enough, for any thing they durst attempt upon us, no more than when we passed the house they were in. And truly, had we acted any thing like soldiers, we had drawn up in the enclosures of each side the narrow deep lane, and there pitched our colours: then we had secured our rear-guard, and have been able to defend ourselves against as many thousands as they were hundreds, upon the advantage we could have made. But we were more like men infatuated; for we had neither [*pass*] word nor [*field*] sign, though we knew the enemy to be in our rear, which caused so great a confusion amongst us, that we fell foul one upon another in the streets, when the enemy came no further than the lane's end where they charged us; and so we beat one another out of the most hopeful design that ever we had in England.

When all our hopes of risings, or any good to be done in or about London, were at an end, then I took a journey (tho' never so ill provided for it,) to Newcastle, to see what the Scots would do; and

[1] The insurrection at Kingston, which cost the Earl of Holland his life on the scaffold, was rashly undertaken, and carelessly conducted. His levies were surprised at their rendezvous, between Evril and Non-Such Park, dispersed and routed, almost without resistance. [*W.S.*]

[2] Lord Francis Villars [*Villiers*], brother to the witty Duke of Buckingham, a youth of a comely person and high spirit. He refused quarter, and was slain by some obscure hand [*W.S.*]

by that time I came there, there was an order of Parliament sent to the Scots, that they should not entertain into their army any that formerly had served the King. But a while after, in the extremity I was in to subsist and by my attempts to get to the town, to find a friend, I was seized upon for a malignant, and sent with a file of musketeers before the Mayor of Newcastle (who was an exact fanatic,) and lays it to me thus: 'Well, had it pleased God to give you victory over us, as it pleased his Divine will to give us victory over you, ye had called us villains, traitors, sons of whores; nay, you had kicked us too.' 'You are in the right on't, sir,' said I: at which he sullenly ruminated, whilst some of his Aldermen could not contain themselves for laughter; but being both of one opinion as to the point, he only banished me the town, with a promise, that when I came again, he would accommodate me with a lodging, which was to be in the Castle-dungeon, where many brave fellows, that came upon the same account as I did, in the hope the Scots would declare for the King, were starved to death by a reprobate Marshal.[1]

The Author's adventures till his arrival in Holland.

When I had waited a tedious time, up and down about Newcastle, in penance to know what the Scots would do; and in conclusion, all to prove stark nought, then I designed to go for Holland. In the mean time, some of the Scots officers very kindly invited me with them into Scotland, assuring me, that from thence were frequent opportunities for Holland: whereupon I went with them as far as Bogygeeth,[2]

[1] Newcastle's mayor in 1645 was Henry Dawson, merchant and mercer. His two brothers also held this office, William in 1649 and George in 1650. In 1647 the mayor was Thomas Ledgerd (sheriff 1622). In *Men of Mark 'twixt Tyne and Tweed* (1895) Richard Welford writes: 'Among those who adhered to the side of Parliament and directed Puritan movements during the Civil War, [were] three members of the local family of Dawson . . . They were followed by a mayor of the same political colour, Thomas Ledgerd, under whose auspices a petition . . . was sent to Parliament, supporting the army and asking that "full exemplary justice be done upon the great incendaries of the kingdom".' Other mayors were: 1645, John Blaxton; 1648, Thomas Bonner. (For this information I am indebted to the City Librarian, Mr W. Tynemouth.)

[2] Bog-of-Gicht, the principal seat of the Marquis of Huntley [*sic*]. That noble person had suffered imprisonment, on account of his loyalty, ever since December 1647, and was finally beheaded at Edinburgh, 16th March 1649. His castle and estates were at present in the hands of his old feudal enemy, the Marquis of Argyle, a man not unlikely to exercise on the depressed cavaliers those severities which his own estate and clan had experienced from Montrose in those unhappy troubles. [*W.S.*]

the Marquis of Huntley's house, in the Highlands, where I saw so much of inhumanity and cruelty executed upon loyal personas, that I had not the patience to stay any longer amongst them, but desired Captain Symrel[1] and Captain Whitehead (my very great friends) to procure a pass for me, which David Lesley refused to give. Then Major Meldrum, (one very much a gentleman, and a soldier,) was concerned at it, and went with me to him, and told him, that he could not in honour deny a gentleman his pass who was invited into their country by some of his own officers, and had engaged their lives for his behaviour. Upon this, Lesley, grinning, told me, 'Sir, you never served on our side.' I told him, 'No, sir, nor never will.' Then he bid me go as I came: and so I had my dispatch, only took leave of those who had no better devotion for him than I had: and then I marched onwards towards Edenbrough; and when I came on this side of it, something near Seaton-House, I was so put to it for want of monies, that I was glad, rather than fail, to take up my quarters in a church-porch, which I was not so much troubled at, to lie all night upon the bare stones amongst the dead, as I was to want something to eat before I had lain down, for I was upon short commons the day before. The next day after I was early up, soon dressed, and a great way to go; and my study was where to be entertained in the day, for I knew well enough where to go at night, as long as churches were in my way: and I had not gone above a mile, but met with some real friends of my old acquaintance, who were more glad to see me bear it so well in that condition, than sparing to assist me upon the account that brought me into that country, and took me with them back to Edenbrough, to recompense me with a better night's lodging than I had the night before; and there accidentally met with a sea-officer of my acquaintance, who told me of a great design he was upon of doing the King service, which he would impart to me when we came aboard, if I would go with him; and when we came aboard of a passage-boat, bound for Cathnes, in the Highlands, he discovered his design unto me, which was so very ill a thing, that no good could attend it; but, with a small persuasion, he declined it. And when we

[1] Symrel is spelled in imitation of the Scots pronunciation of the proper name, Somerville, sounding the letter *v* as an open *u*. The officer here named seems to be James Somerville of Drum, ancestor of Lord Somerville, who then served in the Scottish army. See his history in the *Memorie of the Somervilles*, vol. II. He is stated by his son and biographer, to have been always a loyalist at heart; and was probably well-disposed to patronise a distressed officer in Captain Gwyn's condition. [*W.S.*]

arrived at the Week in Cathnes, I had enough of Captain Smith's designs; and by a match of jumping I made with one John a Groat, a skipper, I gained my passage back to Edenbrough. From thence I travelled to Newcastle, from thence to London, from thence to Graves-end, and from thence, with much ado, to get to sea, where I thought never to have any more to do at land, for the conjuring storms we were in, but by a great providence that we arrived at Serick Seas[1] in Holland, where I had some repose: yet I was always solely devoted never to rest anywhere, no longer than your Majesty had any commands for me, and I to have my health, limbs, and liberty: therefore I went again and again into Scotland, before I had done with it.

[1] Zurick-Zee. [*W.S.*]

II

The King's execution filled Montrose with a fierce resolve to continue the struggle on behalf of his martyred master. Many Royalists were at The Hague. A sensation was caused by the assassination of Dr Isaac Dorislaus, the Parliamentary ambassador. Gwyn was in Amsterdam at about this period, and, learning that Montrose intended to resume the struggle, he enlisted under the Earl of Kinnoull who in August 1649 led an advance party of 80 officers and some Danish recruits. This, in itself, sheds new light on the campaign. They landed in September in the Orkneys where the Earl's uncle, Lord Morton, was governor. Montrose, who was in supreme command as viceroy and admiral of the Scottish seas, was detained in Scandinavia, but the following January joined the force. It was the Marquis's last adventure. Gwyn's account of it is disappointingly brief. He does not appear to have witnessed the fatal conflict at Carbisdale where on 27 April 1650 the Covenant troops under Colonel Strachan scattered the Royalists. The Marquis, discarding the coat adorned with the Garter star he had recently received, escaped to the wild moors where for two days he wandered without food. Taking shelter in the house of Neil Macleod, laird of Assynt, he found himself betrayed. It is possible that Gwyn was serving with the reserve under Colonel Grahame who retired to their base in the Orkneys. Gwyn's account is redeemed by his suggestion that a raid to rescue Montrose, which they 'might easily have done', could have saved the situation. Stranded in Kirkwell, Gwyn escaped in a Dutch fishing vessel—'a herring bus'—which carried him famished to Amsterdam. John Buchan asserts that Gwyn is 'almost our only authority for the Orkney part of the campaign' (Montrose, p. 351 n.).

How strangely carried were some of Marquess Montros his affairs in Holland, which was in order to his last engagement into Scotland: and likewise his public concern in the general, were managed before and after his arrival in the Highlands, until unhappily he was betrayed into the hands of his mortal enemies.

The Author engages in Montrose's service.

At Amsterdam, before he went over into Scotland with the Earl of Kaynoole, upon Marquess Montros his engagement, I was told by those who condoled us, (as knowing our business better than some of ourselves did,) that we were all betrayed; and by our proceedings it appeared to be so, as thus: first, we were to have a small fleet vessel,

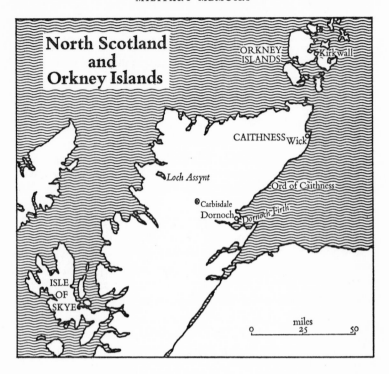

North Scotland
and
Orkney Islands

ORKNEY
ISLANDS

Kirkwall

CAITHNESS Wick

Loch Assynt

Ord of Caithness

Carbisdale

Dornoch

Dornoch Firth

ISLE
OF
SKYE

miles
0   25   50

with twelve guns; and, instead of that, we had an old one, new vamped, without a gun; then we were chased at sea by a Parliament frigate, which the tempestuous weather kept off, and as that might soon fail us, we were prepared, as knowing the worst, to receive our doom bravely, with an attempt to board the enemy, sink or swim; or had there been ever so many of them, we were all resolved, with the Earl of Kaynoole, in that desperate condition, rather to be buried alive with our swords in our hands, than die any other way less honourable, and more cruelly, at their choice; and when, through the extremity of continued storms, we arrived (as Providence would have it) at our port, there had been, for three weeks, three more Parliament men-of-war, impatient at our long coming; and, at that very hour we came, they went some other course to look us, as though we were not out of sight; but as the evening drew on, and the fog which arose obscured us, when we came secure ashore.[1]

[1] Montrose, in his last ill-fated expedition, landed in the Orkneys, where he recruited his handful of forces by a compulsory levy among the unwarlike islanders. [*W.S.*]

Message from Lesley to Kinool, and his answer.

A while after that we were in quarters in those several islands of
Orkney, David Lesley was sent with a considerable force of horse and
foot to suppress us: and before he came to the water side, which he
was to cross over first, sent a packet to the Earl of Kynoole, and,
amongst other circumstances, declared, that by all the obligation and
interest that ever was between them, the best service he could do to
his Lordship, was to advise him speedily to make his retreat into some
other country; for his orders were to be severely executed upon him
and his party; which my Lord Kaynoole, received with so much
indignation, that he commanded the packet to be burnt under the
gallows, by the hand of the hangman; and his Lordship himself was
to see it done. Upon this so public and general a defiance, David
Lesley presently prosecutes in his commands; and when he had
boarded several boats-full of horse and foot, to come and fall upon us,
there arose so great and sudden a storm, that they could not stir,
before another strange relief came, by a counter command sent to
Lesley, that wherever it reached him he was to quit all former orders,
and forthwith to return and march to the west against a greater invasion there; which at last proved to be but false alarum, whatsoever
the design was, more then to divert them from us, and to give us a
longer respite in the country.

Earl of Kinnoule's death.

About two months after, the Earl of Kynoole fell sick at Bursey, the
Earl of Murton's [*Morton's*] house, and there died of a pleurisy, whose
loss was very much lamented, as he was truly honourable and
perfectly loyal.[1]

Sir John Hurrey attacks the enemy at the Pass of Ord.

When Marquess of Montros arrived amongst us into Orkney, and had
settled affairs as he thought most expedient in those several islands he

[1] The author is here at singular variance with the Scottish genealogists. William, third
Earl of Kinnoul, is by them represented as having succeeded his father in 1644. It is
agreed on all hands, that he was a loyalist, and joined Montrose. But far from repre-
senting him as dead in 1650, the date of Montrose's last and fatal expedition, he is stated
to have escaped from the Castle of Edinburgh in 1654, and having instantly joined
Middleton, (in which case Gwyn must again have met with him,) there to have been
taken by the English in the Braes of Angus, and finally to have died in 1677. [*W.S.*]

crossed over into Cathnes, in the Highlands, where, in two or three
days after, our Major-General, Sir John Hurrey, went with a party of
three hundred foot, to engage an enemy treble his number, at a pass
called the Ord, which they thought to maintain and oppose us in our
march. This pass is a steep hill, with a strong river at the bottom of it,
which we waded through, and scrambled up the hill in disorder, that
the enemy, upon these several great advantages, might have done so
great an execution upon us, as few or none should have gone to tell
what became of the rest: but they had not the patience to stay so long
and do it, for the haste they were in to be gone, as most of them were
no soldiers, but country bumpkins, there called Whigs.[1]

*Colonel [Henry] Grymes [Grahame][2] retreats into Orkney, upon the
defeat of Montrose.*

Soon after, Montros marched further into the Highlands, and
Colonel Grymes (his natural brother) was coming up with a recruit of
five hundred more men to him, and were come something near the
place where he was defeated which made Colonel Grymes to retreat,
and march back into Orkney, where one Sir William Jonson[3] was left
governor: and upon a debate amongst them what best to do, they
only talked (and that was all,) as if they would go by sea, and rescue
Montros, which they easily might have done, as there was no fear of
an enemy thereabout, since the party of horse which beat him had
done their work, and were gone far enough from those parts, and
himself in the custody of a pretended old friend,[4] who had few or no

[1] Not from sour-milk, as is somewhere alleged, but from the cry of the West Country
horse-dealers to their trains of horses. To *Whig*, is to make haste. Hence 'Whig-away,'
and 'Whig-amore' was the usual cry of those country-jockies, who bequeathed their
name to a numerous political party. The insurrection of the Ayrshire Presbyterians, who
expelled the Commission of Estates from Edinburgh in 1648, was called the Whigamore's
Raid. [*W.S.*]

[2] Grahame often pronounced, on the English Border, Grime. [*W.S.*]

[3] Mis-spelled for Johnson. Bishop Wishart notices amongst Montrose's followers,
'Henry Grahame, the Marquis's own natural brother;' and 'Colonel Johnson, an old and
resolute officer'. We learn from the same authority, that these two gentlemen were left
almost defenceless in the town of Kirkwall. [*W.S.*]

[4] Montrose was taken by Neil M'Leod of Assint, who having been one of the Marquis's
followers, hesitated for a time what course to pursue; but at length, partly from fear,
and partly from the lucre of four hundred bolls of oatmeal, he delivered up his gallant
general to Lesley's soldiers. [*W.S.*]

more for a guard upon him than were the family and servants of the house wherein he was in restraint, and in a manner concealed too, until there came forth a declaration, that whosoever should apprehend and secure him, should have such a sum of money for his reward: but, in the mean time, had we done any thing, we could not have done less than endeavour to fetch him off; having had time enough, and to spare, for it, and the house he was in so very near the sea,[1] as an opportunity offered for it: but the governor of Orkney choosed rather to take some of the merchants' ships out of their harbour to carry himself, and others whom he pleased, away with him, leaving some of us behind a sacrifice to Lesley, and others our foes in the country. Howsoever, I met with the best of the worst luck, for, by a kindness which I had done not long before to a grateful person, came so home to me as to preserve me strangely; and my last fair escape was an opportunity to get in an open boat for Shetland, and from thence in a herring-bus for Holland, when your Majesty was under sail for Scotland.

The Author returns to Scotland. A diverting adventure.

In Holland[2] I have always made my condition with the officers, not to stay (nor did not,) when there was any thing stirring of action for my King; and at my return from Montros his engagement, and unhappy defeat, the next occasion which offered itself was General Midleton's engagement likewise into Scotland, with whom I went, notwithstanding my great weakness after a severe fit of sickness, and the extremity I had run through twice in that country before: yet all signified no more with me (in comparison) than it is with a woman in labour; for I as soon forgot it, from the great devotion I ever had to persist in my loyal duty: and when we came to the Fly, and stayed

[1] The Castle of Ardvrach, the seat of Neil M'Leod of Assint, seems the place alluded to. It is situated on the north side of the loch of Assint, a large salt-water lake, and may have been liable to such surprisal as our author hints at. But it seems improbable that Montrose remained there long enough after his defeat to have given Johnson time to have embarked from Kirkwall and doubled the northern extremity of Scotland. Another scheme for the liberation of the gallant Marquis had nearly succeeded. At the house of Grange, where he quartered for a night, the lady so 'drugged the possets' of his guards that they all slept soundly, while Montrose, in a lady's dress, passed through amongst them, and was only discerned, and stopped by one of the outposts, where the sentinel had not had his share of liquor. See the *Memorie of the Somervilles*, and the *Memoirs of Montrose*, Edit. 1819, p. 380. [*W.S.*]

[2] The first Dutch War broke out in May 1652.

there three or four days, seven or eight of us being in quarters at a Scotts house, where the man, wife and daughter, were possessed [*convinced*] (against all gainsayings) that the King was in disguise amongst us; and for the conceit sake that such a thing might be, and to humour their fancy in it, we put Mr Ball, a proper handsome person, who they took for the King, to sit in a great chair in the parlour, over against the door, which we had locked, and took out the key designingly, that they might relieve one another in peeping into the key-hole, as they did, and saw how we attended him with all the ceremonies imaginable; and when he thought fit, gave us a sign with hand to be covered; then we put on our hats, to null all distinction, and became familiar comrades as before: A while after the door was open, the mother and daughter, with the goodman, lagging in the rear, came, supplicating [*a*] few of us standing at the street-door, that he and they might have the honour to kiss the King's hand, since he despised not the meanness of his entertainment in so poor a subject's house as he was pleased to come into. We told them it was strange how they came to know it; but since it was so, if they would be conjured to silence, and not speak on't, they should; whereupon they replied that they would rather die than divulge it: and presently they went to uncase, and put on their best clothes, which (in a manner) was as soon done as at three motions, for haste to kiss the King's hand. The goodman led into the room, in a trembling awe, the mother and daughter filed after melting in tears, and on both knees kissed his hand, and wheeled away with abundance of satisfaction. A short while after, as we were going to dinner, there were several sorts of wine privately conveyed into [*the*] room for us; and when we had eaten plentiful, and drunk in abundance, Mr Ball grew heavy and drowsy that he went to lie down: the goodwife observing him, presently commands her daughter to go wait upon him, and know if he wanted for any thing; and upon her stay something extraordinary, the mother tells us, 'Truly, gentlemen, if my daughter proves with bairn, the child shall not want for the cost:' but at parture, they were highly troubled that he would not accept of those rings and jewels, which they purchased at so dear a rate, to present him, as a token that he would be pleased to remember them when he came to his kingdom.

In the autumn of 1653 Gwyn paid yet another visit to Scotland. This time he enlisted under the veteran Middleton who had served the Parliamentary cause. After participating in the Earl of Glencairn's expedition, he sailed a second time from Holland to carry ammunition to Scotland, and wintered in Caithness. Information is scanty and Gwyn's most valuable contribution (though brief) is his reference to the duel between Glencairn and Sir George Monro, who arrived as Middleton's second-in-command. Glencairn, brave though he was, found the task of preserving order beyond him and relinquished the post to the more experienced Middleton. Gwyn refers a number of times to Captain Jack Gwilliams, a comrade in Holland and Flanders. Gwilliams was a Roman Catholic and had helped to defend Raglan Castle. In addition to being in Holland, he served in France, Ireland and Scotland before he joined the Royal Regiment of Guards in Flanders. As a Roman Catholic he resigned his commission in the regiment on 25 September 1667 and was reappointed Captain on 25 March 1672, but resigned again the following year. Gwyn seems to have shown no animosity at the scheme to get Gwilliams posted in the place which he considered was due to his seniority.

The Author passes the winter in Caithness.

When we left the Fly, and were under sail, we had a fair passage without any kind of disturbance; that we arrived safe into the Highlands of Scotland, lodged our artillery and ammunition at an old castle called Skeebo, (or Skelbo,) where we stayed for some days, until the general, with some few with him, had gone up further into the country; then he sent for us, and put us into winter quarters in Cathnes, and thereabouts.

Difference between Earl of Clinkern [Glencairn] and Monro.

In the spring of the year, about May, General Midleton and the Earl of Clinkern met in a town in the Highlands, called Dornach, where Clinkern was to resign all former commands unto Lord Midleton; and before they all parted that night, Lieutenant-General Monrow and Clinkern chanced to clash, and the next day fought, which proved very ominous and unhappy; for it created factions and animosities amongst them, in so much that it was conceived to be the greatest obstruction of any thing whatsoever to the ruin of that design; for, in a short time after, we rather decreased than increased, and were chased up and down the Highlands by General Munke and Morgan,[1] who were a great many too many for us; and we did not care how seldom we see them, especially since little Morgan gave

[1] See J. W. Fortescue, *History of the British Army*, vol. I, pp. 253-5.

us a brush; then we wheeled any way to avoid them, as if that had been true what I heard say there and in England since, that our orders were not to fight: which I was apt to believe, when we neglected such impregnable passes, and rather seemed to draw them after us further and further into the country, as if that had been our chief design, and not to engage them; but whatsoever it was, it presaged not well with so ill a beginning.

The Author, in the Highlands, escapes from the enemy by means of a shower.

Towards the later end of the year we returned for Cathnes, after we had dropped a great many by the way, and marched from thence towards my Lord Rey's [*Reay's*] country, with the enemy pursuing us flank and rear: but when our small forces came half a league beyond Thursaw, (a town in the Highlands,) they marched through a river in a happy shower of rain, which the small rivulets that came from the hills thereabouts swelled so big and strong, that the enemy could not pursue us any further for that part of the day; so by that means we got so much the start of them, and kept it till we came to a rendezvous, in the middest of great hills, and there we disbanded, every man to shift for himself, which I was less able to do, being so very lame as I was: but my Lord Nappier,[1] my constant great friend, was so concerned with my condition, that he was pleased to recommend me to be with my Lord Rey for that winter season; and the next summer it was my fortune, in his Lordship's view, to do him acceptable service against his enemy.

At Stranaver, in the Highlands of Scotland, when my Lord Rey sent to burn his house, lest the enemy that landed should possess it, being upon their march towards it, I urged to have nothing burnt; but, if his Lordship would hazard his party of fourscore men with me, I would meet that three hundred approaching enemy, and beat them; which I did so effectually, that this country was not at all reduced under the subjection of the usurped Commonwealth.[2]

[1] Archibald, second Lord Napier, nephew of the great Marquis of Montrose, to whom he was so much attached, that they were said to be as inseparable as the Pope and the Church. He partook of all his uncle's victories and dangers, and died in Holland, just before the Revolution. [*W.S.*]

[2] Your Majesty had a report of this at Collaine [*Cologne*]. Captain Gwilliams, late of the royal regiment of Guards, can attest this. [*J.G.*]

This passage, which must belong here, has been transferred from Part IV of the *Memoirs*.

The Author returns to Holland with General Middleton.

From Stranaver, Captain Breams, Captain Gwilliams, Captain Richardson, and myself, marched to the Isle of Skye, to the Laird of Macloud's [*MacLeod's*] house where the General was, and where we continued, until he took an opportunity to be shipped for Holland, and a troublesome passage we had of it.

And of two hundred officers, reformados, and gentlemen, that went over with the General, not one of them stayed so long as to return with him but myself.

The Author's Verses against Monro.[1]

General Midleton, in a discourse at Mackloud's house, did very much reflect upon the unworthiness of his Lieutenant-General Monrow; to which replied Captain Gwilliams, that Captain Gwyn displayed him in his right colours, in a few lines he made in answer to the libellous lines thrown upon the Lords that deserted Midleton, though they stayed whilst there was any hope or likelihood of doing any good.

The General was pleased to ask of me if I had those lines about me. I told him yes; and presented them unto him as herein written:

> Was not Monrow amongst us? What needs then
> To cite the smaller crimes of other men?
> Since he so grand a traitor proved, as though
> Himself, by beat of drum, proclaimed it so.
>
> To confirm the world, how that treason can
> Destroy an army, by a single man,—
> You'll easy read, in his prodigious face,
> His coming fatal to a loyal place.

In the original quarto edition the second portion of the book contains an account by an anonymous author[2] *of 'The Earl of Glencairn's expedition as*

[1] Sir George Munro, who fought a duel with Glencairn, whom he appears to have insulted most gratuitously, was bred in the Low Country wars. He was amongst the officers employed by the Scottish Committee of Estates; but afterwards turned Royalist, like Middleton and others. In Balcarras's *Account of Scots Affairs at the Revolution* Sir George Munro is mentioned as having been present at the head of the Militia in 1688, although he had 'lost everything which he had learned in Germany long ago'; and retained only 'affected nastiness, brutality, and fanaticism'. [*W.S.*]

[2] Scott considered that the narrative was written by 'John Graham of Ducrie, a gallant soldier'.

General of His Majesty's Forces to the Highlands of Scotland in the years 1653 and 1654'. This contains an eye-witness's account of the incident which resulted in the duel between Glencairn and Monro to which Gwyn refers. The account begins in August 1653 when Lord Glencairn met the chiefs of some of the clans who promised to bring forces to participate in the expedition. Colonel Blackader headed thirty horsemen. A description is given of the gathering of the clans and the efforts made by the Parliamentary general, Major-General (Sir) Thomas Morgan, to scatter them. When Lord Middleton arrived to take over the army, Lord Glencairn went to Dornoch to receive him. The account continues as follows:

'*The army being drawn out in order, Lord Glencairn went through every regiment of horse and foot, and informed them all that he had now no longer any other command than as a private Colonel. . . . After this, the General Middleton did entertain them all in his quarters. Then Lord Glencairn invited him, and his General Officers and Colonels, to dine with him at Kettle, a house four miles south of Dornoch, the headquarters. His Lordship gave them as good cheer as the country could afford, and made them all very hearty. After dinner, he called for a glass of wine, and expressed himself to this purpose to the General: "You see, my Lord, what a gallant army I, and these noble gentlemen with me, have raised out of nothing. They have hazarded their lives and fortunes to serve his Majesty. Your Excellency ought therefore to give them all the encouragement you can." Immediately Sir George Monro started from his seat, and interrupting Lord Glencairn, said, "By God, the men you speak of are no other than a pack of thieves and robbers. In a short time I will shew you other sort of men." Glengary started up, thinking himself most concerned; but Lord Glencairn stopped him, and said, "Forbear, Glengary, 'tis I that am levelled at": and directing himself to Monro, told him he was a base liar; for they were neither thieves nor rogues; but much better than he could raise. General Middleton commanded them both to keep the peace; and addressing them said, "My Lord, and you, Sir George, this is not the way to do the King service, to fall out among yourselves: therefore, I will have you both to be friends:" and calling for wine, said, "My Lord Glencairn, I think you did the greatest wrong in calling Sir George a liar,—you shall drink to him, and he shall pledge you"; which the noble and good Lord did without hesitation. Sir George, after his old haughty humour, muttered some words which were not heard, and neither pledged him nor drank to him. The General then ordered his company to horse. Lord Glencairn would have conveyed him to the head-quarters, but his Excellency would not allow him to go farther than a mile. So he returned to his quarters with Colonel Blackader and John Graham of Deuchrie.*

He became exceeding merry on his returning home, and caused the Laird's daughter to play on the virginals, and all the servants to dance. Just as he was going to supper, Alexander Monro, brother to Sir George, called at the gate, when his Lordship commanded immediately to let him in, and saluted him at the hall-door as being very welcome, and made him sup with him, placing him at the head of table next the Laird's daughter. The whole company were very merry. Immediately after supper, he told Monro that he would give him a spring if he would dance; and accordingly he did, the Laird's daughter playing. While the rest were dancing, his Lordship stepped aside to the window, and Monro followed. They did not speak a dozen words together. My Lord called for a glass of wine, and drank to him; said he feared he would be too late to go to the head-quarters. As soon as he was gone, he called for candles and went to bed. Blackader and Deuchrie lay in the same room with his Lordship. As soon as he went to his room, the whole family went to bed. None was privy to my Lord's design but John White, his Lordship's trumpeter and his valet. It was agreed, that as the nights were short, my Lord should meet Monro half way between Dornock and his quarters, by grey day-light; so that my Lord got not two hours' rest; and though the two foresaid gentlemen lay in the room with him, he went out to the field and returned without their knowledge. None went with him but his trumpeter; and Monro came with none but his brother the Lieutenant-Colonel. They were both well mounted on horse-back; each of them were to have one pistol; after discharging of which, they were to fight with broadswords. The pistols were fired without doing hurt. They then engaged with their swords; and after a few passes my Lord had the good fortune to give Sir George a sore stroke on his bridle-hand; where-upon Sir George cried out that he was not able to command his horse; "and I hope", says he, "you will fight me on foot". "Ye carle," says my Lord, "I will let you know that I am a match for you either on foot or on horse-back." Whereupon they both alighted; and at the first bout, my Lord gave him a sore stroke on the brow, about an inch above his eyes, which bled so much that he could not see. His Lordship was going to thrust him through the body; but John White, his man, pushed up his sword, and said, "You have enough of him, my Lord". His Lordship, in a passion, gave John a stroke over the shoulders, and then took his horse and came to his quarters. Monro and his brother went to the head-quarters, but with much ado, for the blooding at head and hand.

'The General being informed of this affair, instantly sent Captain Ochtrie Campbell to secure Lord Glencairn in his quarters, which was done before six in the morning. The manner of securing him was by taking his *sword, and commanding him to be arrested in his chamber, and taking his parole not to disobey the General's order. This happened on Sunday morning.*

'. . . Sir George carried so high, that no reconcilement was to be had betwixt my Lord and him. So his Lordship, on that day fortnight after the duel was fought, which was on Sunday, set out for the south. He took no more but his own troop with him, and some gentlemen volunteers that were waiting for command; in all about 100 horse. . . .'

III

The year 1657 saw Gwyn in wholly new surroundings—one of the band of exiled Cavaliers who had joined the army of Charles II and served under the banner of Spain. Cromwell had fought the Spaniards at sea; he now meant to fight them on land; hence his alliance with France. By treaty he agreed to send six foot regiments (6,000 men) to the Spanish Netherlands. The campaign was to capture three fortified coastal towns: Mardyck, Dunkirk and Gravelines. The English navy under Montague was off the coast. For this support Cromwell was to receive the two former towns which he desired to use as bases to command the Straits. Marshal Turenne was in supreme command.

In the Spanish army were five Royalist regiments: three Irish (the Duke of York's, Lord Ormonde's and Lord Bristol's), one Scottish (Middleton's), and one English, (some 400 strong), composed mainly of men of quality. This was the Royal Regiment of Guards under the Earl of Rochester in which Gwyn was a lieutenant. A sixth regiment under the Duke of Gloucester had been captured earlier in the year.

Gwyn loses no time in pointing out that the King made him a lieutenant in the Royal Regiment of Guards. This is confirmed by a list of officers sent to Charles II by his colonel, the Earl of Rochester, which includes the name of 'Capt. John Gwine, Lt.' His company commander was Colonel William Slaughter, killed at the Battle of the Dunes.

The Memoirs touch on the preliminary manoeuvres. After Cambrai had been threatened by Turenne, the French marched to the coast to unite with the redcoats who had landed in June. Mardyck, lightly held by the Spanish, was easily taken by the French who, in accordance with the agreement, handed it to the English. The Spanish army, led by Condé, Caracena and Don John, appeared before Ardres on 27 August. Miners were leisurely sent forward to prepare for the assault. An easy capture was anticipated and a report that Turenne was advancing to the relief of the town was ignored. When, the next day, this was found to be correct, the siege was immediately raised, the troops being withdrawn with little loss. The Spaniards made for Gravelines.

At the Battle of the Dunes (3 June 1658) Royalist and Roundhead fought each other in a foreign land for a foreign cause. The six regiments of Roundhead redcoats bore the brunt of the battle, led by Gwyn's old enemy of the Highlands, Major-General Sir Thomas Morgan. King Charles II and his brothers, the Dukes of York and Gloucester, were with the Spanish army. Morgan's men charged up the sandhills and cleared them of Spaniards—it was then that

Colonel Slaughter was killed. The Duke of York tried to check the rout by charging with his troop of horse, but in vain. A group of several hundred men was left amid the sand dunes. It was the Royal Regiment of Guards.

The Author in Flanders was made Lieutenant in the Royal Guards.

In Flanders your Majesty was pleased to make me one of the first Lieutenants in the Royal Regiment of Guards; and the first small action we were upon was against Mardick, where we went to know what we should do when we came next; for then we did nothing to our advantage, as was publicly known.

I was at the siege of Ardes [*Ardres 27–29 August 1657*], where we stayed not so long as to do any good against it, before the French came to the relief of it; and we were so loath to leave it, that at last we came trotting away.

Antwerp blockaded by Carasien.[1]

I was at the most regular fortified and pleasant city of Antwerpt, where the Magistrates, merchants and burghers of it opposed General Carasien, for his unworthy, base exaction, and obstructing their ancient customs and privileges, which before were ever preserved inviolably, and of an exceeding great concern to them; but yet, for all that severity and grand abuse put upon them, they at last recollected themselves, and had so much wit in their anger, as to consider, that so potent an army was too apparent too many for them; and therefore; per force, must submit, according to an old saying, 'Might overcomes right': which inclined them, of necessity, to make the best of the worst as to comply with them, and purchase their peace at a dear rate from him, who was obliged to protect them, and not oppress them.

Description of Antwerp, and Account of Carasien.

And their army did them a great and an unknown damage as they were quartered in their most rarely contrived gardens and houses of pleasure, hardly to be paralleled for all kinds of delights and private recreation, which was conceived to be superabundant, and so magnificent for them, by Carasien, who greatly envied their happiness, since he (slim devil) had no such conveniency, or choice places, to buckle with his miss, he made shift to get with child in the hollow tree in Brussells Park, and most perfidiously, (as it was in his nature,) broke his vows and protestations with her, to such an odium, that she, poor lady, for ever after renounced to have any more to do with man for his rogue's trick, and turned nun upon't. Carasien was but a private captain when he rid in the hollow tree.

Flanders.

With three hundred foot I convoyed a boat, with ammunition, from Ghent to Courtrey, notwithstanding that I was challenged at the river-side by a guard of the enemy, and the French camp within half a league; but with an advantage of the night, and my contrivance, I marched with an appearance of several great bodies of men more then my number; ready to fight; that they at that instant would not

---

[1] The Marquis de Caracena, a leading Spanish general.

engage, but brought their whole army a little too late to do it, that I arrived safe.[1]

The Author's account of the action at Dunkirk [3 June 1658].

I was at Dunkirk fight, when Marshal Turen raised his siege, to come and give us battle on the sand-hills; and well he might, having so much the odds of his side as his own army of infantry to spare, unless what he did against the brave Prince of Cundey [Condé]; for the English and Swiss had the van and onset of that day, which totally routed the Spanish foot and the Spanish cavalry, (for the most part of them,) when they thought themselves overmatched, when they saw they were overnumbered, faced about in time, leaving them to fight that had a mind to it: but his Royal Highness the Duke of York [in a] most eminent and memorable action upon the English left wing,[2] drew them off from falling upon us, to make up the great breach he had made amongst them; and their reserve of horse, commanded by Marquess Ramboor [Rambures] of Brittany, were advancing upon us, till he understood we were English; then from the great tenderness he owned to have unto your Majesty's concern, as knowing who we were, commanded one of his Captains to come and tender honourable conditions unto us, with high applause for our resolution to stand the field when all had left us. When his Royal Highness engaged on our right wing, the Swiss on their right wing were at the same instant engaged with a regiment or two of Spaniards, to whose assistance a troop of horse came briskly up to charge the Swiss: they received the volley-shot, and instead of falling in with sword and pistol, wheeled to the left, away they went and came no more.

The Duke of York has described the incident:

'But none of these misadventures did at all daunt the King's Regiment: they continued to stand firm, and maintained their ground, though they

---

[1] There are yet some soldiers surviving, in the Royal Regiment of Guards, can aver this. [J.G.]

This passage, which belongs to this period, has been transferred from Part IV.

[2] There is an excellent and candid account of the battle of Dunkirk in the *Memoirs of James II*, of whom the first General in the world (Wellington) has been heard to say, that he writes of military matters more forcibly and intelligibly than any author whom he has perused. [W.S.]

beheld *the first line of the French passing by them on their left hand, and the Cromwellian English on their right, till the second line came up to them. It was the Regiment of Rambures which advanced to charge them (their Colonel commanding that line, and being at their head). This officer seeing not a man standing of all our troops, excepting this small body which was before him, went up to them himself, a little before his men, to offer them quarter; to whom they returned this answer, that they had been posted there by the Duke, and therefore were resolved to maintain that ground as long as they were able: he replied, that it would be to no purpose for them to stand out, their whole army being already routed, and having left the field. They answered again, that it was not their part to believe an enemy: upon which he offered them, that if they would send out an officer or two, he would himself carry them up to a sand-hill which was behind them, and then they should perceive, that what he affirmed was true: accordingly they sent out two officers, Captain Thom: Cooke and Aston [or Ashton], whom he conducted as he had promised to the sand-hill which he had named; from whence they could easily discover, that none of our army was left standing except only themselves, after which, he brought them down again to their own men, whereupon they told him, that in case he would promise they should not be delivered up to the English, nor be stripped nor have their pockets searched, they would lay down their arms and yield themselves his prisoners; to which he immediately agreeing, and giving his word for the performance of those articles, they accordingly yielded, and his promise was exactly kept to them. . . .'*[1]

The Author taken prisoner.[2]

Colonel [*William*] Careles,[3] Major [*John*] Beversham, Ensign Crispe, Mr Rudston, our chirurgeon, and myself, went with the Captain that came and tendered conditions unto us; and the rest of the regiment had better come with us, then go away in parcels as they did, to the great sorrow of some, and the death of several.

His kind reception by the French.

And when, upon hearty welcome, we had helped the Captain eat

---

[1] *The Memoirs of James II* (Chatto and Windus, 1961), p. 272.

[2] At the Battle of the Dunes.

[3] Colonel Careless will be remembered for the part he played in the escape of Charles II after the Battle of Worcester (3 September 1651).

up all the provision he had at present, he very worthily treated us at the vivandière's; supplied us with monies for the time we stayed, for a convenient opportunity to be gone; let us go upon our own parole; contracted with us for half ransom; and in the night conveyed us, with a small party of horse, through the camp without the line; directed us how to avoid the out-sentinels, and, like a brave Briton as he was, to crown the rest of his civilities with the last, produced whole clusters of bottles of wine from under some of their cloaks, which we sacrificed in the remembrance of princes, till we were almost all so in conceit, and fortified us purely to neglect those great water plashes we waded through, and the broad deep ditches, brimful, we moiled over, sometimes near diving with want of lopestaves; and when we arrived at Newport [*Nieuport*], to present ourselves and our condition unto his Royal Highness the Duke of York, we had the happiness to see him safe preserved from the eminent danger he had been in amongst his enemies.[1]

Gallantry of some Private Soldiers.

I cannot omit an unparalleled devotion expressed by eighteen or twenty private soldiers, (questionless all gentlemen,) who came not with whom we had made condition; but, by a mistake, unluckily fell into the hands of rather fellows and hedge-birds, then any men of the mind of soldiers, as to cut, strip, and mangle them, at an inhuman rate, being disarmed prisoners of war, and then left at the ruins of an old house, where one of General Morgan's men told me they were, I found them: and upon my desire to know how they came to be so barbarously used, told me, because they would not part with their new clothes which troubled them, not so much for the want of them to cover their nakedness in that extremity they were in, but as they were the King's gift unto them, which they prized as their lives.

The same continued.

And their bravery, above all, was that when their old English officers

---

[1] Although the Duke of York was then engaged on the side of the Spaniards, yet when there was a rumour that he had fallen into the hands of the republican English, then the allies of France, Monsieur de Gudagin, who commanded the French infantry, traversed the field of battle with a select body, determined, should the Prince be prisoner amongst his father's enemies, that he would rescue him out of their hands, either by fair meanes or by actual force. *Memoirs of James II*, vol. I, p. 360 [*W.S.*]

(from whom they first came to us),[1] were to see them, told them, they all knew very well what it was to run away from their colours, especially to a foreign people, to come and fight against their country, friends, and relations; but howsoever all should be kindly waived by the general and his officers, if they would return to their former colours; and likewise, all would be forgiven and forgotten, and care taken for the recovery of them, as if the prejudice they received, had been in their own country's service. They told them plainly, that they never served them with any devotion, but merely for an opportunity to come and serve their own King; and, since their sad fate would not permit them to live and serve him, in spite of fate they would die his martyrs, rather than renounce their allegiance.

The Author commanded to Ipres [Ypres].

Soon after the battle, I was commanded, with ten men, a sergeant, and a corporal, to go with a party of three hundred Irish, to wait upon the Prince Delin's [*de Ligne's*] commands at Iper; and when we had been there a while, he marched, with four thousand men into the country upon a design, and had not gone far, but an enemy was like to surprise him in his march; which made him counter-march it back to Iper sooner than he thought, or was expected.

The Author's ill-treatment, and remarks thereon.

And were ten men, a sergeant, and a corporal, a proper command for a commission-officer, then, in all reason, either Gwilliams, Munson, Broughton or some other inferior officer, ought to have gone, and not I, that was a prisoner upon parole. I understood their design was to give Gwilliams an opportunity to make his interest to get the company to which I was lieutenant, my captain [*having been*] killed in the field, and myself a prisoner at the head of my command: yet, I repined not, since your Majesty was pleased to tell me, that, had you remembered me to be Colonel Slaughter's lieutenant, no man had come over my head: nor none did thereafter; for I had the next two succeeding vacancies, which were Colonel Gross his company

---

[1] Those, to wit, who were in the service of the Republic or Protector, under whom, it seems, these men had served, and from whom they had escaped into the service of the King. [*W.S.*]

and Sir Richard Maulevers', when persons of great interest and quality could not obtain either.

The Author's generosity.

After we had been twelve or fourteen weeks upon extraordinary commands at Iper, we were as far from receiving any money, to enable us for service, as commonly [we] were used to be, save only a half-pennyworth of bread for twenty-four hours, and that when we could catch it; so that we lived upon as near to nothing, and as much upon the fresh air, as most poor men alive could do. But at last, there was privately conveyed into my hand five week's bread-money, due unto us in arrears since we came into the town, with advice to make use of it myself, and pay it when I could better spare it, and the party to have more need of it; for now they all lived well upon the spoil. I was both sensible and glad of it; but yet I called my sergeant aside, and gave him the money, bid him pay himself and the party, and withal to desire them from me that they tell not the Irish soldiers of it, lest they mutter against their officers, why they had not their money as well as we ours; but the party's kindness was above their secrets to me, for they could not conceal, but must needs divulge that which they so much approved of to be so real and justly done; when, on the contrary, others of their officers kept their money from them, and sent them abroad a-begging, which was so frequent in the English and Irish mouths, as never to be forgotten.

Remarks on the foregoing passage.

This subtle contrived march was fixed upon me unavoidably; for, had I refused to go, then they had highly exclaimed and informed against me for a grand mutineer, as not to obey command: and, on the other side, if I had been taken in arms, a prisoner upon parole, I had been hanged without mercy: but I rather choosed to take the hazard of hanging than disobey command, though never so unjust as that was: and it's well known, I never was anywhere upon command, but I did something which was acceptable, if anything was to be done: and, I presume, I may justly say, that I have gone a volunteer out of complaisance to brave men, and love to my King's service, as often against the enemy and successed as well as some of my adversaries can brag to have been, in all their time of action in his Majesty's service. And

I would waive all their injustice to me, if any of them, in their under-takings, can parallel what here in this manuscript I make to appear on [*one*] side of a leaf.

An unhappy accident.

And my paying of the party their bread-money, when it looked insignificant whether I did it or not; and their often repeating it amongst themselves and the Irish, hath created a great kindness for me amongst them all, and proved a happy fortune for those who perhaps little think on't now, and preserved other lives upon an occasion soon after; for when we returned from Iper to our quarters, by Ghent, it happened that an Irish sergeant, and three or four Irish soldiers with him, were coming by us, would have taken a hatchet from our lad, that was cleaving of wood upon the door-sill, who would not part with it, but flung it into the room amongst the soldiers; and they, who would as soon die as part with that which kept them alive, went out and fought them, killed the sergeant, who fell not amongst them, but carried himself to a hedge hard by, there dropped and died: and our soldiers knew not but that he was got away as well as the rest, till Colonel Leg [*Legge*] came by, and saw him there dead; sent for me, told me, that 'this unhappy thing must needs be done by some of your men;' and desired that his body might be carried into the house; and it being a market day at Ghent, some of them might come drunk by, and see him killed, might incense others of them to do mischief; and withal desired, that no man touch his body, for, to his knowledge, there was a charge of gold about him: and, as soon as the corps was brought into the house, I told the soldiers that they presently barricade the doors, and make ready their arms, for I expected them to come for a revenge: and so there came some three hundred of them, about an hour or two in the night, run against the door, thought to surprise us, and so take their revenge but could not enter: whereupon I called to them; when I called to them I told them my name; told them that I came that evening off the guard from amongst them: and likewise told them, that Colonel Leg required me to suffer none to go out of the house till an account be given who killed the sergeant; and desired them to offer no violence, for to be sure they should have right done them the next day. But, as good fortune would have it, the major part of those men went and came from Iper with us so lately, that made them presently to reflect

94

upon what they knew I had done of right to my soldiers there and elsewhere, and did not attempt any further, but satisfied themselves and the rest of them with that I had told them: and some of them openly declared, that they would rather stand in my defence than offer the least prejudice wherein I was concerned: and about 10 or 11 of the clock at night, came Major Farel [*Farrell*], with a commanded party, by order of a council of war, to demand right for what was done; but the circumstances between us tended not to much more than what was done the next day, for the business was examined, determined, and the men cleared.

And it may easily be conceived, that some three hundred men would have been too hard upon a dispute for nine or ten which were in an old country cottage, had it not been for their forbearance, (and that was for my sake,) and, upon the least disgust, were resolved to take leave and be gone; then we could have no winter-quarters, and without it there had been no regiment.

Further sufferings at Nivelles.

When we were in quarters at Nivel, we were a tedious time without money by the corruption of officers, who kept wholly to themselves the route-money due unto us from Doway [*Douai*] to Antwerpt; sold the canteen of wine and beer; and likewise sold the bread-money: and when they had converted to their own use that little we had to keep life and soul together, in consideration of it gave the soldiers passes to go up and down the country a-begging; and, to remove so great a scandal, seven or eight of us met one evening to advise upon't, and were resolved to prepare a petition how unhappy we were exposed of so long a time, and to send it enclosed in a letter to some honourable person at court that we could make our friend, to present it unto your Majesty. This being put upon me to do, the next morning, before I came abroad, I had done the petition, (and more than was expected or mentioned ere night amongst us,) writ a letter to our lieutenant-colonel, why we made an address to any other person then himself, to move your Majesty in our behalf; and another to my Lord Wentworth, who above all others, I pitched upon to make our friend, as my letter herein relates. When all was done and approved of, not only by those officers, but by [*Colonel Matthew*] Wise himself, yet he would not have sent them away, because (as he told us) the King's orders were on the way, coming to fetch us over for England: but it came not in two or three months after.

A copy of the letter I writ to my Lord Wentworth in behalf of the regiment.

Right Honourable,

We hope there needs no apology to this truth, that the very best news we have heard from England since the King's most happy Restoration, (as to our concern,) is, that your Lordship commands his Majesty's Royal Regiment of Guards, for we are confident in your prudent care and justice done to us upon all occasions; and truly at this present, our condition highly implores the assistance of some noble friend; and we know not to whom so well to make our humble address, to present and second this enclosed unto his Majesty, than to your Honour, since report and our hope, speak you our Colonel. My Lord, we are left scarce one part of four whom at Dunkirk battle entirely devoted themselves to be sacrificed for our King's sake, rather than deceive his reposed confidence in the resolve of his too few (at that time) loyal subjects. But, having escaped the worst, beyond our hope as to be prisoners, three parts of us perished with a tedious imprisonment and want of bread, and the few remainder here languish as having no allowance to live. This our insupportable condition, the character of your Lordship's wonted nobleness to assist an honest cause that wanted a friend, and the interest we are encouraged to have in your Lordship, very much persuades us of your kindness and condolence. But if, through mistake, (as necessity occasions many,) we herein presume more than [we] ought, we hope that necessity will plead an acceptable excuse to so noble a spirit.

General Carasien's ill-behaviour at Namur.

When we removed our quarters from Neevell to Namures, General Carasien sent his orders before to the magistrates and burghers of the town, to let them know that the King of Britain's Regiment of Guards was coming to quarter there; and that they were to give them no other accommodation than vacant houses upon the rampart and court of guards; and were to expect their whole subsistence from their own King, being restored to three kingdoms. This was not according to our service to the King of Spain, when Carasien quit the field, and left us there, to deserve better from his master than himself did at that time: and, had it not been for one of his Royal

Highness the Duke of York's gentlemen Mr Dutell, a native there-abouts, that gave us credit for bread, it had gone very severe with us, as having neither money, friends, or relations to relieve us; but as Providence sent us this person, and not long after, came there a letter from my Lord Wentworth, out of London, to prop our hope, assuring us that he was our colonel; and advised us, as he was sensible of our condition, to write a petition unto your Majesty, with the officers' hands to it; then to send it enclosed in a letter to him, and he would present and second it unto your Majesty. When this I had done, it was perused, approved, and subscribed accordingly. Whereupon I told them, 'Gentlemen, I hope now you will think it expedient to write unto my Lord Wentworth.' 'No,' said [Col. Matthew] Wise; 'I will send the petition in a letter to Brussells, for Jack Gwilliams to send to Colonel Wheeler.' I told them, that Colonel Wheeler was my great friend, and a person whom I much honoured; but yet I could not justly put him in competition with my Lord Wentworth, who is our colonel, whose kind and obliging letter was by us to be observed, rather as a command from him: besides, he is a noble person, a Privy Councillor, and can speak with the King when the other cannot; and make our addresses more acceptable unto his Majesty. But, right or wrong, Wise was resolved to send the petition, that it might come to Wheeler's hand. Whereupon I went away, and would not own to be one that should put so great an affront upon so honourable a person, and being my colonel too: but I left the petition amongst them, to do what they pleased with it. This was ground enough for Wise to incense Wheeler at what rate he pleased, against me; that Wheeler, and others amongst them, made me as odious to my Lord Wentworth, that he would not hear me speak for myself, nor no man else for me: but I may safely swear, he little thought then that my justifying of his Lordship's priority and honour, upon a debate amongst us, whether the petition, written by his own orders and direction, should be sent to him, or to his lieutenant-colonel, was the occasion that provoked him to so great an anger against me, and to suffer my ruin to ensue upon't, after I had, with much ado, survived so many hazards and sorrow in my King's service.

The Author prevents a mutiny at Nivelles.

When we were in quarters, in vacant houses, not far from Neeval, some of my soldiers one morning came to me, grievously sharp set, and in that hungry humour sadly complains of the hard measure they had, as to be forced to beg, steal, or starve, which was not always to be done, nor would they do it any longer; vowing, that it was for my sake they stayed there so long languishing at that rate. I could not take any thing ill that eased them with talking, because to be sure, whatsoever they begged, stole, or made a shift for, I had my share of it, or I might have gone and do as they did, or not live; therefore I seemed to comply with them, to gain their patience but to the next day; and, in the mean time, I would fix upon something commendable for us all to do in so great an exigence; and so prevailed with them. After we had parted, I was in a heavy loss with myself what fallacy I should use next, having so often before deceived them with such fruitless stories: but when I had pitched upon what I thought would best suit with the humour of brave fellows, I put it in black and white what I would have them with me to resolve upon. The next day, I went to them and told them, 'Gentlemen, I am come to make good my promise unto you; but first, I must tell you, that whereas you talked yesterday of starving, I presume you will all allow that I know best what it is, since upon Amsterdam iron-bridge, after I had come from Montros his engagement, I sunk down dead with mere hunger; and had it not been for the great charity of strangers that revived me, I had gone (for ought I know) the way of all flesh, insensible of any further pain; and, besides, you all know very well, that not long since I was in quarters, with Colonel Careles, his lieutenant, and others, and truly we had no other choice for our Christmas-day dinner, then a well-grown young fat dog, as cleanly dressed, and as finely roasted, as any man need put into his belly: and we had no need to complain, since we had not anything to feed upon as was man's meat; nor need you want such novelty now; and then, if you do but look well about ye when you go abroad a-preying, whilst there is a care taken for a better accommodation for us. In the mean time, let's all resolve, with a brave old saying, 'What can not be cured must be endured;' for we came here to live and die in the King's service without scrupling; but like gentlemen and soldiers,

> We'll here in point of honour starve, and try
> How long we'll pine with hunger ere we die.

The next section picks up the story immediately after the Restoration when, peace having been declared, soldiers who served in the Royalist army and

*those who had been Parliamentarians, found themselves doing garrison duty
together. The possibility of difficult situations arising is obvious. Colonel
Wise, acting as a senior company commander is a reminder of the manner
in which officers, regardless of previous rank, were glad to get employment
which would avert starvation. The governor would have been Sir William
Lockhart.*

Colonel Wise's behaviour to the Author at Dunkirk.

When Dunkirk came to be your Majesty's town and garrison, the
Regiment of Guards came first to quarter there, and the officers but
upon half-pay; yet, notwithstanding that, I proposed amongst them,
that it was proper some of us should go wait upon the Governor and
desire that he would be pleased to appoint a parade-place for us in
case of an alarum, that we might draw up, stand to our arms, and be
in a readiness if any commands should come,—which they did not
approve of: and when a strong alarum, at break of day, with drums
beating, clattering and jangling of bells, as if the enemy were at the
town's end; then of a sudden I made myself ready, and repaired alone
to the Governor, who I found alone in his chamber, and desired to
know of him if he had any commands for those few remainder of his
Majesty's Regiment of Guards. He very kindly received me, and told
me we should be very welcome, and be very glad of our company.
Whereupon I made haste away, and sent my sergeant to let Colonel
Wise know what the Governor had told me, whilst I run up and down
the quarters, to get the soldiers in as much readiness as possibly I
could; and, for want of a parade-place, gave them orders to draw up
against Wise his quarters, as he was eldest captain, and all our field-
officers absent, which the soldiers observed: and when I came there
myself, sent several times to Wise to know what his orders would
be; but he neither came nor sent, but let us go as we came at; which
I was something concerned, and spoke to Ensign Sackfield [*Sackville*],
and Ensign Stoner [*Stonor*], my familiar associates, and told them,
that they very well knew the soldiers of the garrison were some of
them who kept to beat us out of our country: and asked of them, if
they would take their fortune with me that day, and we would go
volunteers to wait upon the Governor, that he and all of them should
see that we were as forward as they, and to go as far as he pleased to
lead us. They told me, 'With all their hearts.' Then I went with them
to the Governor, as he was marching at the head of fifteen hundred

men, and told him they were officers of his Majesty's Regiment of Guards, gentlemen, and brave fellows; and that they and myself would own it an honour to take our pikes upon our shoulders, and wait upon him that day. He returned as many grateful expressions unto us, as if it had been the highest obligation that ever was put upon him, and would not take us from our command.

IV

Part IV comprises merely seven sections and here appears even smaller as several 'chapters' have been removed and placed in their proper chronological order. Of this part the most remarkable section is Gwyn's expression of gratitude to Speaker William Lenthall who was so conspicuous in the House during these momentous years. It obviously concerns one of the conspiracies in which Gwyn was involved. The question is—which? It was probably one which presaged the Restoration. In 1654 Lenthall was set aside as Speaker in favour of Francis Rouse, provost of Eton, former M.P. for Truro—a step which was obviously little to Lenthall's liking. Again, in October 1659, a couple of months after Lambert had suppressed Booth's Rebellion, Lenthall, who had been reinstated by the Rump, was arrested as his coach arrived at the House (presumably by Lambert's orders) and he was instructed to return to his home. It is possible that by this time Lenthall had foreseen that the only way to bring peace to the troubled country was to recall the King. He aided in bringing about the Restoration. Gwyn evidently considered it advantageous to hint that he had played his part in influencing this change of heart in the great Parliamentary Speaker. His comments throw a shaft of light on a little known aspect of the times. Lenthall died in 1662.

The gratitude of the Author to Mr Speaker Lenthall.

That I have been courted by a seeming great enemy, in those days, (when my betters were sold a groat a-dozen,) to stay with him, upon the account of what service he would do unto your Majesty, if there should come a revolution amongst them, as they expected it; I was sick in my mind to know, whether or no I might confide in him, but did not: yet, for the exceeding obligation he put upon me for those few days I was at his house; and, as sometimes there are retaliations of civilities from one enemy to another, so, after several years absence, and when your Majesty was at Oxford, the troop of Guards at Abingdon,[1] and I there then upon my crutches, I could not rest satisfied until I had writ a grateful letter unto Mr Lentall, as an acknowledgement of those favours I received in the worst of times, for such men as I was. A copy of which letter I do here insert, as the nearest witness I have to affirm what I allege:

[1] Gwyn evidently served in His Majesty's Own Life Guard of Horse after the Restoration.

Sir,

You know it an old saying, and so often affirmed, that 'One mischief pursues the other:' Nor have I, for these months that I broke my leg, met with anything so much to trouble me, as that I cannot come with the first to pay my respects, and kiss your hand, being so near the place where I received my obligation, (or rather, a blessing, in that age;) but I shall leave it unto these my worthy comrades, to make my apology, as they know best; only thus much be pleased to take from me, that there is neither hedge nor ditch between this and your fair mansion, but I could cheerfully scale on my crutches to come and wait upon you, were it in the least requisite to express the devotion and honour I have for you. In the mean time, until I receive your commands, or meet with anything called your concern, wherein, if need, I may act a grateful part, I will publish your merits where I have credit, and create servants unto you, of such gentlemen and brave fellows, whom never had the honour to know you, but from [*the text breaks off here*].

Conclusion

I could add very much to this small Manuscript, of what else has been my observation, besides my own undertakings and performances, if I thought requisite; but I will rather reduce the total of what more I have to say briefly thus: I never objected against any difficulties, whatsoever I should meet in going to any place or country to serve my Prince; but was always one of the very first upon all engagements; and have been at as many fights, small and great parties, desperate sallies, and private engagements, as any one man's time could permit: nor can any just person say, to his knowledge, that ever he knew me to act anything unworthy an honest man, a gentleman and a soldier. And I hope, that this real account of my fidelity and service, with the severity and hard measure dealt me, (unknown before unto your Majesty,) will render me the more acceptable unto your Majesty's most gracious and wonted promise of reward; and as it may encourage others to proffer their duty and service to their King equal, (or above their lives;) as, for example, those eighteen or twenty brave fellows did, at Dunkirk battle, or as that small party from the Devizes have expressed it, when they courageously sung and fought till they routed Waller's rear-guard at Marlbrough town, and with a jovial old tune, which here brings up the rear.

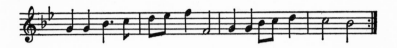

Appendix I

Gwyn's prefatory letters were to:

1. King Charles II (see p. 45)
2. The Duke of York
3. The Duke of Monmouth

To his Grace the Duke of Monmouth.

Sir,

This small manuscript is in obedience to your Grace's late commands, and an account unto the King of my time spent in his service, where I have not only been a spectator to what was done, but so frequent upon action, as to gain the experience to know my own resolution so far, that before I would be surprised by a neglect of your Grace's commands, being my General, my Captain, so great a master in arms, and already so famous in heroic actions, I would choose rather to do as an old comrade of mine (one Aldersey) has done; who went but little way from his command, in the interim, the enemy fell upon his post, and cut off most of his men, before he returned and desperately ran in amongst them with his sword in his hand, embroiling in blood, till they had mastered him with wounds, and offered him quarter, which he refused to take, saying, 'I will not outlive the day that shall make me be hanged for neglect of duty,'—and so fought to death, as it was really rendered unto him.

Your Grace's most humble servant and
  Soldier, to command,
   JOHN GWYN.

4. The Duke of Buckingham
Gwyn reminds his patron that 'before the late intestine wars, I had the honour to be known unto your Grace, and receive your commands, when with the royal Princes, ye, all in your infancy, were so earnestly inclined to arms', and speaks of their 'appearing in formal bodies skirmishing and fighting' and their 'brisk firing'—evidence that Gwyn had played a part in their training.

5. The Duke of Albemarle, the Captain-General
6. The Duke of Grafton
7. The Earl of Pembroke
In this letter Gwyn describes his wounds as 'the marks which makes me weather-wise'.
8. The Earl of . . .
Gwyn speaks of 'more than six times seven years' service to my King, both at home and abroad'.
9. The Board of Green Cloth

To the Right Honourable his Majesty's Officers of the Board of Green Cloth.

Were I invested in the command which is well known to be justly my right, I should now (at least) be the third field-officer in the royal regiment of Guards, who daily have the honour to guard his Majesty's sacred person, the Royal Family, and their most honourable household: or had I attained to whatsoever of command above my merits, yet truly I should ever own it a first fair step to preferment for me to have been bred in the nursery of your young clerks at Court; for they were always hopeful in their employs, as were their successive advancements honourable. Nor knew I any of them that repaired to the royal armies, but came as brave and worthily to their commands, as whose ambition were solely devoted to honour and the King's service; and for myself, how I have improved my time, according to my poor talent and trust reposed in me, presented the King, his Royal Highness, and my general, each of them with a small manuscript, whereof this is another of the same, which I humbly offer unto your Honours' kind acceptance as my obligation; having for several years before the late unhappy wars served under your management, to make me capable of succession amongst ye; but for my military engagement, which I was encouraged to by princes, and which I hope you will all approve of, as the perusal of these the loyal endeavours, and real account of
Your Honours' most humble servant,
J.G.

10. Sir John Salusbury
11. Colonel . . .

Appendix II

1642

c. July–Sept.	Commissioned and raised in North Wales
23 Oct.	Battle of Edgehill. In Feilding's tertia: about 1,200 strong
12 Nov.	Storming of Brentford
9 Dec.	Quartered at Reading

1643

16–27 Apr.	Siege of Reading. Departure of Sir Thomas Salusbury: Sir Charles Lloyd given command
May	At Culham Camp, near Abingdon
26 July	Storming of Bristol. In Belasyse's tertia, C.O.: Lieutenant-Colonel Edward Tirwhitt
10 Aug.– 5 Sept.	Siege of Gloucester
20 Sept.	First Battle of Newbury. In Sir Gilbert Gerard's tertia
Autumn	Quartered at Reading

1644

Apr.	At Reading. 409 strong
29 June	Battle of Cropredy Bridge
Aug.–Sept.	The Lostwithiel campaign. In Lisle's tertia
Autumn	Garrisons Devizes
27 Oct.	Second Battle of Newbury. Detachment present under Major Richard Lloyd

1645

Feb.	Capture of Lacock House and Rowden House, Wiltshire
Aug.	Capture of Chippenham. Detachment of fifty present
Aug.	Skirmish at Aldbourne
23 Sept.	Surrender of Devizes Castle after a week's siege Regiment dispersed

Biographical Notes

Horse, Foot and Dragoons are here abbreviated as H, F *and* D.
Prisoner of War as POW

RICHARD ATKYNS

RICHARD ARUNDELL (d. 1687), 1st Baron Arundell of Trerice, 1644.
'A stout and diligent officer' (Clarendon). Fought at Edgehill.
Governor of Pendennis Castle, 1662. (*D.N.B.*)

SIR JACOB ASTLEY (1579–1652). Sgt–Maj.–Gen., *F*, in 'the Oxford
Army', 1642–45. Governor of Reading from about September 1643
to April 1644. Baron, 1645. (*D.N.B.*)

COL. SIR HUMPHREY BENNET. *H, F*. High Sheriff of Hampshire.
Fought at Cheriton and commanded a brigade in April 1644, took
part in the Cornish campaign of 1644, and greatly distinguished himself by a successful charge at Second Newbury. He was in Winchester
when it surrendered on 8 Oct. 1645.

BRISTOL. *See* DIGBY.

GEORGE BRYDGES, 6th Lord Chandos (1620–55). Col. *H*, 19 Nov.
1642. Distinguished himself at First Newbury. Left the Royalist army
in 1644, having ruined his fortune in the King's cause. Heavily fined
by the Parliamentarians. Killed Henry Compton in a duel at Putney,
13 May 1652. Imprisoned for manslaughter. Died of smallpox and was
buried at Sudeley, Gloucestershire. (*D.N.B.*)

COL. BRUTUS BUCK. *F*. Hertford's army. Commanded a tertia at
the storming of Bristol, where he was slain, 1643.

COL. ROBERT BURRILL or BURGHILL. A Scots veteran, may have
been a captain in the Dutch service. Captain, then Major, *H*, 1642.
Did good service in the Forest of Dean and was promoted colonel.
His wounds at Lansdown were probably severe as he does not seem
to have served thereafter.

SIR JOHN CADEMAN (*c.* 1615–*c.* 1645), Physician-General to the Army

of King Charles I. Probably son of Sir Thomas Cademan (*c.* 1590–
1651), Physician to Queen Henrietta Maria, he was a Londoner and
a Doctor of Medicine of Bonn (or Bologna). Extra-licentiate of the
College of Physicians and physician to the army, 1640. Sir John was
beheaded at Bristol for killing an officer there. (*Mercurius Belgicus.*)

SIR HORATIO CAREW or CAREY. Capt. *F*, 1640. Major *H*, Sir
William Waller's Regiment, 1642. Deserted the Parliamentarians in
July 1643 and joined the Royalist Army. Col. *H*, 1643. In the defence
of Bristol, 1645.

CARNARVON. *See* DORMER.

WILLIAM CAVENDISH, Marquis of Newcastle (1592–1676), commanded the Royalist Northern Army from 1642 to 1644. After his
victory at Adwalton Moor, 30 June 1643, he might have marched
south, but instead besieged Hull for six weeks. The siege was raised
on 11 Oct. (*D.N.B.*)

CHANDOS. *See* BRYDGES.

DR JOHN COLE, D.D.(OXON). Rector of Ifield, Sussex, in 1640.
Ejected, 1642. A commissioner for the surrender of the Scilly Islands,
1651. Described by the Rev. Francis Corker, a traitor to the Royalist
cause, as 'a great stickler but a great coward; so that . . . by menaces
you may have anything out of him' (A. G. Matthews, *Walker Revised*
(1948), p. 355). Restored 1660–63.

CRAWFORD. *See* LINDSAY.

ROBERT DEVEREUX, 3rd Earl of Essex (1591–1646). Parliamentarian
general. Commanded at Edgehill and First Newbury. Lost his army
at Lostwithiel. (*D.N.B.*)

GEORGE, LORD DIGBY (1612–77), who became 2nd Earl of Bristol in
1654. (*D.N.B.*)

ROBERT DORMER, 1st Earl of Carnarvon (k. 1643). Served in both
Scots Wars, being Col. *H* in the second one. Col. *H*, 1642. Fought at
Edgehill and Lansdown. Killed at First Newbury. Clarendon tells us
that he 'always charged home' and that he was 'full of honour and
justice'. (*D.N.B.*)

JOHN DUTTON (1594–1657), of Sherborne, Gloucestershire, was an
M.P. for that county, and one of the richest men in England. He sat

in the Oxford Parliament of 1644. 'Crump' Dutton, so-called because of a humped back, was noted for his meekness, prudence, learning, and good works. (M. F. Keeler, *The Long Parliament*.)

ESSEX. *See* DEVEREUX.

FORTH. *See* RUTHVEN.

GRANDISON. *See* VILLIERS.

COL. SIR BEVIL GRENVILE (1596–1643). Knighted at Berwick, 23 June 1639, in the first Scots War. He greatly distinguished himself at Braddock Down and Stratton. He was a man of great influence in Cornwall. (*D.N.B.*)

SIR JAMES HAMILTON. Col. *F*, 1640. In about May 1643 he raised three regiments, *H, F* and *D*, in Worcestershire. His regiment, *H*, was beaten up at Lye on Mendip shortly before Lansdown. Hamilton fought bravely at Worcester in 1651, where he was desperately wounded. In 1657 he was Lt-Col. to Lt-Gen. John Middleton's Scottish Regiment, *F*, with Charles II's army in the Spanish service in the Low Countries.

CAPTAIN HANMER. Probably one of the Flintshire family.

HERTFORD. *See* SEYMOUR.

SIR ARTHUR HESILRIGE (d. 1661). One of the Five Members. Clarendon calls him an 'absurd, bold man'. He fought at Edgehill as a troop commander and later raised his well-known cuirassier regiment, 'the Lobsters'. He had been wounded at Lansdown. The wound Atkyns gave him may have been rather severe, for he was prayed for publicly in the London churches. Some accounts of Roundway Down, not unreasonably, attribute Waller's defeat to Hesilrige's faulty tactics. He fought at Cheriton, and his regiment was at Cropredy Bridge. During Cromwell's invasion of Scotland (1650) he was Governor of Berwick. After the Restoration he was imprisoned in the Tower, where he died. (*D.N.B.*)

RALPH, 1st BARON HOPTON OF STRATTON (1598–1652). One of the most successful Royalist commanders. Defeated the Parliamentarians at Braddock Down, Launceston, Stratton and Lansdown. (*D.N.B.*)

CAPT. EDWARD KITELEY or KYGHLEY (k. 1643). Commanded the 42nd troop of the Parliamentarian Army in 1642.

MAJOR ROBERT LEGGE. A professional soldier, he was cornet to Henry Wilmot (q.v.) in 1641. He was major to Prince Maurice's Regiment, H, from 1643 to 1645, when he was taken prisoner at Evesham. On his release he seems to have become lieutenant-colonel to the regiment of horse commanded by his brother, Colonel William Legge (q.v.), who was then Governor of Oxford.

WILLIAM LEGGE (1609?–70). Served in the Dutch and Swedish armies, and in the Scots Wars. He was Rupert's brigade major as well as major of his regiment, H. He became a colonel in 1645 and Governor of Oxford, vice Sir Henry Gage, who was killed in January of that year. Legge was not actually commissioned as Governor on 7 May 1645. He was dismissed on 14 Sept. 1645 in consequence of Prince Rupert's surrender of Bristol. (D.N.B.)

MAJOR WILLIAM LEIGHTON. Served as a lieutenant in foreign parts before 1639. Major, 1642, the King's Lifeguard F. Fought at Edge-hill, where he is reported to have been wounded, and at the storming of Cirencester. Lt-Col. c. 14 June 1643. Probably fought at both battles of Newbury, at Cropredy Bridge and Lostwithiel. He was not captured at Naseby, where his regiment was destroyed. Knighted, 4 Sept. 1645. He was in the defence of Colchester in 1648, and was in the Tower in 1658–59. Capt. F, King's Regiment of Foot Guards, 17 March 1664–18 Oct. 1665.

WILLIAM LENTHALL (1591–1662), Speaker of the House of Commons. His wife, Atkyns's kinswoman, was Elizabeth, née Evans.

LUDOVIC LINDSAY, 16th Earl of Crawford (1600–52?). He had been a colonel in the Spanish service. He had a distinguished record during the civil wars, both in England and under Montrose in Scotland. He commanded a brigade at Roundway Down. (D.N.B.)

COL. JAMES LONG (1617–92). High Sheriff of Wiltshire, 1624. (D.N.B.)

PRINCE MAURICE (1620–52). A son of Frederick V, the Elector Palatine, and a younger brother of Prince Rupert. (D.N.B.)

LT-COL. GUY MOLESWORTH. Lt F, 1640. Served throughout the First Civil War as lieutenant-colonel of Prince Maurice's Regiment of Horse, being wounded at Roundway Down and Naseby and taken prisoner at Stow-in-the-Wold. After the Restoration he served in Portugal. On 13 June 1667 he was commissioned as major to Lord Alington's Regiment, F, which was disbanded at the Treaty of Breda. In 1669 he petitioned King Charles II for leave to establish a lottery in Ireland.

LT-COL. RICHARD NEVILL, of Billingsbear, Berkshire. Capt. H. Distinguished himself at Newburn 1640, in the Regiment of Lt-Gen. Viscount Conway, 1641. Carnarvon, H, 1642. He succeeded to the command of the Regiment when the Earl was killed at First Newbury. He probably fought at Cheriton, and was slightly wounded at Cropredy Bridge. He was in the Cornish campaign of 1644.

NEWCASTLE. *See* CAVENDISH.

ROCHESTER. *See* WILMOT.

PRINCE RUPERT (1619–82). Count Palatine of the Rhine and Duke of Bavaria, afterwards Duke of Cumberland and Earl of Holderness. At this period he was General of the Horse. (*D.N.B.*)

PATRICK RUTHVEN, Earl of Forth and Brentford (1573?–1651). Lt-Gen. of 'the Oxford Army' 1642–44. (*D.N.B.*)

WILLIAM SEYMOUR, 1st Marquis of Hertford (1588–1660). Lt-Gen. of the Western Counties, 1642. 2nd Duke of Somerset, 1660. (*D.N.B.*)

MAJOR THOMAS SHELDON (d. 1643). Ensign F, 1640. Troop commander, Prince Maurice's Regiment H, 1642. Fought at Edgehill.

COL. SIR NICHOLAS SLANNING (1606–43). Knighted at Nonesuch, 24 Aug. 1632. Governor of Pendennis Castle, 1635. Served in the Scots War, 1639. In 1642 he raised a regiment of volunteers, called 'the Tinners', which fought in all the victories of the Cornish Royalist Army in 1643. (*D.N.B.*)

MAJOR (SIR) PAUL SMITH or SMYTH (*c.* 1606–*c.* 1666). Gentleman of a company under the Earl of Oxford in the Dutch service, 1629. Captain by 1639 when he returned from foreign parts to serve King Charles I. Captain in the Scots Wars 1640–41. POW. Portsmouth. Major, Lord Wilmot's Regiment, H, 1642. Lt-Col., *c.* 20 Sept. 1642 (vice Edward Feilding, k. First Newbury). Served in Cornwall. Slightly wounded at the relief of Banbury, Oct. 1644. Capt. Earl of Rochester's Regiment, in the Low Countries, 1657. Indigent Officer, 1663. Paul Smith received a warrant for £120 as Royal Bounty,

13 Jan. 1664–65 (*Calendar of Treasury Books*, vol. I, 1660–67, p. 645). Sir Paul Smith became Lieutenant in the Duke of Richmond's troop and regiment of 'Select Militia', 2 July 1666. (Dalton, vol. I, p. 61).

COL. JOHN TREVANION. Raised a regiment of volunteers in Cornwall, 1642, and, like Slanning, fought under Hopton in the West.

GEORGE TRYME, of Wookey's Court, Somerset, was Secretary-at-War to the Marquis of Hertford and served Charles I throughout the war—without pay.

MAJOR JONAS VAN DRUSKE. A Dutchman. Lt *H*, Sir Horatio Carey's troop, Waller's Regiment, 1642. Probably became Major to Burghill, whom he seems to have succeeded. Commissary-General *H*, 1644.

WILLIAM VILLIERS, Viscount Grandison (d. 1643). Col. *H*. His regiment fought at Edgehill but was destroyed at Winchester in December. Col.-Gen. *F*. Commanded the first tertia at the storming of Bristol, where he was mortally wounded.

LT-COL. JOSEPH WALL (k. 1643). Sir Humphrey Bennet, *H*.

SIR WILLIAM WALLER (1597?–1668). Parliamentarian general. By his early victories in 1642 and 1643 he earned the nickname of 'William the Conqueror', but he was to lose his army at Roundway Down. His greatest success was at Cheriton. Though defeated at Cropredy Bridge, he commanded the greater part of the Parliamentarian Army at Second Newbury. He is credited with the idea of the New Model Army. His tactical skill was much admired even by his enemies. (*D.N.B.*)

CORNET WASHNAGE. It is likely that this was Cornet George Wastneys, who was in Wilmot's Regiment, *H*, in the second Scots War (1641). He was the third son of Sir Hardolph Wastneys, Bart., and according to family tradition was killed at Devizes after slaying five persons.

LT-COL. SIR ROBERT WELSH. Sir George Vaughan, *H*. Knighted on 24 Oct. 1642 for his part in rescuing the Banner Royal at Edgehill, when Capt.-Lieut. to Wilmot, H. After the Restoration he claimed as an indigent officer, listing himself as a Colonel under Prince Rupert (*A List of [Indigent] Officers, 1663*).

HENRY WILMOT, first Earl of Rochester (1612?–58). Capt. *H*, Dutch service, 1635. Wounded at the siege of Breda, 1637. Sgt-Maj.-Gen. *H*, in the second Scots War. Taken prisoner at Newburn, 1640, though not before he had distinguished himself. Held high commands in the Royalist Army from 1642–44, when he fell into disgrace. His brilliant victory at Roundway Down was his chief exploit. He shared Charles II's adventures in the escape after Worcester. (*D.N.B.*)

SIR HENRY WROTH of Enfield, Middlesex, was a Gentleman Pensioner in 1636. During the First Civil War he served in the Lifeguard of Horse and was knighted at Chirk Castle on 15 Sept. 1645. In 1661 he commanded a troop in the Royal Regiment of Horse, now 'The Blues'. Mrs Hutchinson speaks of his considerate treatment of her husband, Colonel John Hutchinson, during his imprisonment.

JOHN GWYN

SIR ARTHUR ASTON (k. 1649). Sgt-Maj.-Gen. *D*. Served in Russia and with the Poles against the Turks. Fought in the Swedish army at Lutzen. Col. *F* 1640. Knighted 1641. Fought at Edgehill, 1642. Governor of Reading, 1642–43, and of Oxford, 1643–44. He lost his command when his leg was amputated in consequence of a riding accident. He had not been popular for, besides being a Roman Catholic, he was testy and imperious. He was Governor of Drogheda when it was stormed by Cromwell, and had his brains dashed out with his own wooden leg. (*D.N.B.*)

CAPT. THOMAS ASTON or ASHTON. In June 1661 was commanding the 6th company of the King's Regiment of Guards at Dunkirk. Out of the Regiment by 1670. (Dalton, I, 6.)

COL. SIR GEORGE BONCLE or BUNCKLEY (d. 1645). An ingenious gentleman of good Scots family who from his youth applied himself to the knowledge of arms, demonstrating his courage, fidelity and judgment and passing through most of the different ranks, and serving both in the horse and the foot. Major, Sir Thomas Salusbury, *F*, 1642. Served in the Edgehill campaign and in the defence of Reading. Lt-Col., Sir Arthur Aston, *H*, 1643. At First Bristol, July 1643, and, doubtless, First Newbury. Lieutenant-Governor of Oxford when Aston was Governor. Commanded the Regiment at the relief of Basing, Sept. Knighted, 7 Nov. 1644. Granted arms 1645, when he was Colonel, *H* (presumably vice Aston) (British Museum Add. MSS 14294). POW Naseby and died in prison of 'hard usage'.

CAPT.-LT N. BREAMES or BREAMS. Lt-Gen. Middleton's Scottish Regiment, 1657–60.

COL. EDWARD BROUGHTON (k. 1665). Son and heir of Sir Edward Broughton of Marchwiel, Denbighshire, and nephew of Colonel Robert Broughton, in whose regiment of foot he seems to have served in Ireland as a captain (1641). Major to the Prince of Wales's Regiment of Foot (Col. Sir Michael Woodhouse), 1643. Wounded in Lord Capel's attempt on Wem (1643). He is probably the Lt-Col. Broughton, POW at Stow-in-the-Wold (1646). He was Major of King Charles II's Lifeguard, F, at Worcester, 1651. He was taken prisoner in Booth's Rising, and sent to the Gatehouse. It was feared that he would lose his life as he was alleged to have broken his parole, but he escaped by wooing his keeper's daughter! He was knighted in 1663. Mortally wounded in the sea fight against the Dutch, 3 June 1665. At that time he was a captain in the King's Regt of Foot Guards. (See Dalton, pp. 7 and 37, Lists of 1661 and 1664.)

CAPTAIN LORD CAULFIELD. William, 5th Lord Caulfield in the Irish peerage. Survived to serve in the New Model Army, Capt., Col. Richard Graves, H.

COL. WILLIAM CARLOS, CARLOSSE, CARLES or CARELESS (d. 1689), served as a captain in Col. Thomas Leveson's Regiment of Horse, part of the garrison of Dudley Castle. He was governor successively of Lapley House (15 Dec. 1642) and Tong Castle. At Worcester (1651) he was major to Lord Talbot's Regiment of Horse, and after distinguishing himself during the battle, was Charles II's companion in the Royal Oak, escaped to France and was taken into the King's service. Commissioned colonel in 1651 (B.M. Harl. MS 6804. f. 197). In 1657 he was a captain in the Earl of Rochester's Regiment of Foot. In 1660 he petitioned for a commission for ballasting ships in the Thames. (C.P.S.D.) In 1661 he was granted one-third of the tax on hay and straw in London and Westminster, and in 1687 he received a bounty from King James II. (D.N.B.)

COMPTON. See NORTHAMPTON.

COL. SIR WILLIAM COURTNEY. There were two Royalist colonels of this name. This is evidently Sir William Courtney of Bogatt, Hampshire. He had a regiment, F, in Hopton's army by Nov. 1643. He probably went to Faringdon after the fall of Winchester (5 Oct.

1645) at which he was present (Sprigge, p. 132). There he seems to have assumed command of the regiment of Sir Marmaduke Rawdon, F. He acted as Governor of Faringdon Castle during the last siege (though Sir George Lisle may have been the actual Governor), and did not surrender the place until 24 June 1646. At the Restoration he petitioned King Charles II for the Tellership in the Exchequer, the Treasurership of the Navy, or the disposal of the places of Clerks of the Cheque. He mentioned that he had been sequestered and denied the benefit of the articles for the surrender of his garrison. (*C.S.P.D.*, 1660, p. 2.)

CAPT. THOMAS COOKE. Probably the Thomas Cooke, who was Cornet to Capt. Hervye in Lord Conway's Regiment of Horse in the Second Scots War.[1] Served in the Queen's Regiment of Foot in the First Civil War.

COL. RICHARD FEILDING (d. 1650). Served in foreign parts and returned home as a captain in 1639. Col. F, 1640. Commanded a brigade at Edgehill. Disgraced for the surrender of Reading he narrowly escaped execution, and was deprived of the command of his regiment, F. Afterwards commanded the Royalist artillery at Cheriton and succeeded in getting the guns away. Served in the Cornish campaign, 1644, and afterwards commanded *The Constant Reformation* in the fleet under Prince Rupert. He died at Lisbon, his will being witnessed by Col. William Slaughter, later Gwyn's company commander.

CAPT. JOHN GWILLIAMS, GWILLIM or GUILLIM. Entered the King's service at the age of 14 and served as a cornet *H* under the Marquis of Worcester. He was all through the siege of Raglan Castle, one of the last Royalist strongholds to surrender (19 Aug. 1646), and his name is in the list of POWs. Went to France, Ireland and then, with over eighty other English officers, to Spain. There he was imprisoned for forty months for the murder of Antony Ascham, the Parliament's ambassador (1650). He escaped and served in Scotland as a captain under Middleton. In 1657 he was a lieutenant in the Earl of Rochester's Regiment, F, in Flanders. In June 1661 he was captain of the 8th Company of the King's Regiment of Guards at Dunkirk. As a Roman Catholic he was compelled to resign his commission (25 Sept. 1667), but was reappointed captain in the same regiment, 25 March 1672.

[1] MS Muster Roll of 25 March 1641 in the possession of Lord Cottesloe.

He resigned in April 1673, but was still alive on 18 Jan. 1683. (State Papers 29/422.f.112.)

COL. SIR GEORGE LISLE (k. 1648). Served in the Netherlands and in the Scots War. Capt. *F*, 1640, Lord Grandison's Regiment. Lt-Col. *D*, 1642. Fought at Edgehill. Commanded fifty *D* at Chalgrove (18 June 1643). Led 1,000 musketeers at First Newbury, being evidently in favour with Prince Rupert. Succeeded Col. Richard Bolle, killed at Alton (13 Dec. 1643), in command of a regiment, *F*. Fought at Cheriton (29 March 1644), commanded a tertia, or brigade, in the Cornish campaign, and greatly distinguished himself at Second Newbury. Governor of Faringdon 1644–45. Knighted, 1645. His brigade was destroyed at Naseby. In 1648 he played a leading part in the defence of Colchester, and, contrary to the laws of war, was shot after the surrender. (*D.N.B.*)

COL. SIR CHARLES LLOYD (d. 1678). Descended from the ancient line of the Princes of Powys and the son of a soldier, Lloyd served in the Dutch army, where he early showed his skill as a map-maker. He was an ensign by 1632. In the Scots war of 1640 he was a captain *F* in the Earl of Northumberland's Regiment. He served in the Lord-Lieutenant's Regiment in Ireland, 1641–42. In the spring or summer of 1643 he succeeded Sir Thomas Salusbury as colonel of the regiment in which John Gwyn was serving. Since he was also Engineer and Quartermaster-General he was not always present with his regiment. He took part in the Cornish campaign of 1644, and soon after became Governor of Devizes. He was active in Wiltshire during the early part of 1645, but surrendered Devizes Castle to Fairfax after no more than a week's siege. He is said to have died impoverished.

COL. HENRY LUNSFORD (k. 1643). Lt-Col. *F*, 1640, Sir Thomas Lunsford's Regiment. Again Lt-Col. when his brother attempted to re-raise the unit in Somerset, 1642. Distinguished himself at Marshall's Elm, 1 Aug. 1642. Fought at Edgehill and succeeded to the command because Sir Thomas was taken there. In the defence of Reading, 1643. Led the foot in Prince Rupert's Chalgrove Raid, 17–18 June. Killed at the storming of Bristol, 26 July 1643.

MANCHESTER. *See* MONTAGU.

COL. SIR RICHARD MAULEVERER (1623?–75). Of Allerton, Yorkshire. Son of Sir Thomas Mauleverer (d. 1655). Admitted of Gray's

Inn, 1641; knighted 28 March 1645. Taken prisoner at the surrender of Colchester, 1648; fined by Parliament, 1649, and his estates sequestered 1650. Outlawed, 1654. Taken prisoner, 1655, but escaped to the Hague. Gentleman of the Privy Chamber, 1660. M.P. for Boroughbridge, 1661. (*D.N.B.*)

JOHN MIDDLETON, 1st Earl of Middleton (1619–74). Began his military career as a pikeman in Hepburn's Regiment in the service of France, but at the age of 20 was already a major in the army of the Covenanters. Lt-Gen. *H*, in the Parliamentarian Army. Changed sides and fought with 'the Engagers' at Preston, 1648; POW at Worcester, 1651. Escaped from the Tower to France. Went to Scotland as Captain-General but his force was dispersed by Monck (1654). Earl, 1656. Governor of Tangier, where he died. (*D.N.B.*)

EDWARD MONTAGU, 2nd Earl of Manchester (1602–71). Commander of the Parliamentarian Army of the Eastern Association. No soldier. (*D.N.B.*)

CAPTAIN LORD NAPIER. Nephew of Montrose. Captain in Middleton's Scottish Regiment in King Charles II's army, 1657.

NORTHAMPTON, James Compton, 3rd Earl of (1622–81). Fought at Edgehill and Hopton Heath (19 March 1643), succeeding his father, killed at the latter place, in command of his regiments of horse and foot. Won the action at Middleton Cheney (6 May). Fought at First Newbury (1643) and became a brigadier early in 1644. Distinguished himself at Cropredy Bridge, served in the Cornish campaign and raised the siege of Banbury Castle (25 Oct. 1644). Routed by Cromwell at Islip after a two hours' fight (15 Apr. 1645), he retrieved his reputation at Naseby where his support enabled Prince Rupert to dispose of Ireton's wing. Though an excellent cavalry commander there is evidence that he was somewhat autocratic. He quarrelled with his brothers and resigned his commands early in 1646.

COL. SIR RICHARD PAGE (d. 1657). A professional soldier of obscure origin, served as a captain in the foot regiment commanded successively by Sir William and Sir James Pennyman. Therefore he probably fought at Edgehill, and Cropredy Bridge. He was certainly with the regiment in Cornwall and received rapid promotion towards the end of 1644. In October the lieutenant-colonel surrendered and Page succeeded him. Soon after Sir James Pennyman also retired and it

was as a colonel that Page led the regiment at the storming of Lei-
cester (30 May 1645), for which he was knighted (2 June). He was
also granted arms in 1645.[1] He was captured at Naseby when the
regiment was destroyed (14 June). Sir Richard Page's name appears
in an undated list of those dieted and lodged at King Charles II's
house in 'Bruxelles' (c. 1656?).[2] He is said to have died in great poverty
at the Hague (1657).

LT-COL. WILLIAM ROSEWELL. Apothecary, of the Old Bailey,
London and North Curry, Somerset. Captain, Sir Marmaduke
Rawdon, F, 16 June 1643. POW, 7 May 1644, at Basing and sent to
Farnham. Major, c. 26 Sept. Distinguished himself in a sortie from
Basing House, 9 Nov. Lt-Col. in the defence of Faringdon Castle, in
Sir William Courtney's Regiment, F. Compounded on the articles
of Faringdon, 22 Sept. 1646. Apparently became a Justice after the
Restoration.

SIR THOMAS SALUSBURY, 2nd baronet of Lleweni near Denbigh.
M.P. for shire in Short Parliament. Chosen by a joint meeting of
gentry of Denbigh and Flint counties as colonel of a regiment of foot
they raised in Aug. 1642 for the King. Followed Charles from Shrews-
bury and fought at Edgehill, receiving an honorary DCL on reaching
Oxford. His regiment led the storming of Brentford then went into
garrison at Reading where they remained until surrender. He does
not seem to have been present at that time as that spring Salusbury
was in Worcester where he appears to have ridden with his troop of
horse, thereby receiving from his chaplain an admonition for neglect-
ing his foot regiment. His death in July (?) is a mystery. Pennant
asserts, 'He retired to Lleweni. His regiment was taken over by [Sir]
Charles Lloyd.'

COL. SIR THOMAS SANDYS, Bart. Colonel of Horse, 12 April 1643.
In Oct. 1645 he was commanding part of Prince Maurice's Lifeguard
(Symonds). Lieutenant in King Charles II's Lifeguard, 1661.

COL. WILLIAM SLAUGHTER (d. 1658). Raised a regiment of foot in
South Wales early in 1645. Fought in Goring's army at Langport
(10 July 1645). Signed the articles for the surrender of Pendennis
Castle, 16 Aug. 1646. Witnessed the will of Col. Richard Feilding

[1] BM. Add. 14294.

[2] PRO. SP. 29/42/53.

(*q.v.*), who died at Lisbon in 1650. Gwyn's company commander in the Guards. Killed at the battle of Dunkirk Dunes.

CAPT.-LT JOHN STRODE (d. 1686). Doubtless served in the Civil Wars, but his services there have not come to light. Lt-Governor of Dover Castle, 1660, but was still captain of 9 Company of the King's Regiment of Guards, *F*, at Dunkirk, June 1661. Was made Major, 28 Aug. 1678. 1st Foot Guards. Described as Col. John Strode. Lt-Col. 1 Jan. 1682. Died 25 March 1686. (Dalton, vol. I.)

COL. ANTHONY THELWALL. One of the Thelwalls of Plas-y-ward, near Ruthin, according to Lloyd's *Memoirs* (p. 661). He may have been a younger brother of Col. John Thelwall. Served in the Rochelle expedition (1628) and in Germany before returning to England as a major (1639) to take part in the Scots Wars. In 1640 he was major of Col. Richard Feilding's regiment of foot, and in 1642 lt-col. to Sir Edward Fitton, whom he succeeded about July 1643. He distinguished himself by his leadership at the storming of Bristol (26 July) and had a narrow escape when a bullet hit the bar of his head-piece, hurting him slightly. Symonds mentions his good service at Cropredy Bridge. He served in the Cornish campaign of 1644. Although he is said to have fallen at Second Newbury, he seems to have been alive in 1648. (*C.S.P.D.*)

COL. SIR JOHN URRY or HURREY (d. 1650). Of Pitfichie, Aberdeenshire. Soldier of fortune. Served abroad. In the Parliamentarian army at Edgehill, but deserted to the Royalists and fought at Chalgrove Field (18 June 1643), being knighted for his services on that occasion. Sgt-Maj.-Gen. of the Horse to Prince Rupert at Marston Moor (1644), where he did not distinguish himself. Deserted to the Parliamentarians just before Second Newbury. Routed by Montrose at Auldearn, 1645. With the Duke of Hamilton's army, 'the Engagers', at Preston, 1648. Escaped to the continent. Major-General to Montrose at Carbisdale where he was taken. Beheaded at Edinburgh. (*D.N.B.*)

COL. SIR CHARLES WHELER, Bart. (1620–83). Of Birdingbury, Warwickshire. M.A. Cantab. Served as a major in the garrison of Newark-on-Trent during the First Civil War and was known for his gallantry. In 1661 Col. Charles Wheler was lt-col. of the King's Regt of Guards at Dunkirk. Succeeded to a baronetcy on the death of a cousin 1666. In 1666–67 he commanded a troop of horse. M.P. for Cambridge University, 1667–79. Colonel of a regiment of foot,

16 Feb. 1678. He was also Governor of the Leeward Islands at one time.

COL. MATTHEW WISE. In 1644 he was Major of a Brigade in Newcastle's army (BM. Harleian MSS. 6804.f.197), and he is probably the Major Wise taken prisoner at Marston Moor (BM.E 54/8). Early in 1645 he raised a regiment of foot in South Wales and fought in Goring's Army at Langport. He was one of the defenders of Pendennis Castle, 1646. He served in King Charles II's army, 1657–61, and was in command of 4 Company of the King's Regt of Guards, F, at Dunkirk in June 1661. (Dalton, I, 6.)

Bibliography

RICHARD ATKYNS

BYRON, SIR JOHN. 'Account of Roundway Down', *Journal of the Society for Army Historical Research*, 1953.

Calendar of the State Papers, Domestic Series (C.P.S.D.)

CLARENDON, EARL OF. *The History of the Great Rebellion*, ed. W. D. Macray. Oxford, 1888.

DALTON, CHARLES. *English Army Lists and Commission Registers*. London, 1892.

GODWIN, REV. G. N. *The Civil War in Hampshire*. Revised edn. London, 1904.

HAMPER, WILLIAM. *The Life, Diary and Correspondence of Sir William Dugdale*. London, 1872.

HOPTON, RALPH, LORD. *Bellum Civile*, ed. C. E. H. Chadwyck Healey. Somerset Record Society, 1902.

A List of [Indigent] Officers. London, 1663. (A copy in S.P. 29/68.)

Mercurius Aulicus. Oxford, 1643.

Parliament Scout. London, 1643.

PEACOCK, EDWARD. *Army Lists of the Roundheads and Cavaliers*. 2nd edn. London, 1894.

SLINGSBY, COL. WALTER. For his accounts of Lansdown and Roundway Down, see HOPTON.

SPRIGGE, JOSHUA. *Anglia Rediviva*, ed. C. E. Long. London, 1647.

SYMONDS, RICHARD. *Diary*. Camden Society, 1859.

— MS notebook. British Museum, Harleian MS 986.

WALKER, SIR EDWARD. *Historical Discourses*. London, 1705.

WARBURTON, ELIOT. *Memoirs of Prince Rupert and the Cavaliers.* London, 1849.

WASHBOURN, JOHN. *Bibliotheca Gloucestrensis.* Gloucester, 1823.

JOHN GWYN

BUCHAN, JOHN. *Montrose.* London, 1928.

— *Cromwell.* London, 1934.

BURNE and YOUNG. *The Great Civil War 1642–46.* London, 1959.

Calendar of Wynn (of Gwydir) Papers. National Library of Wales, Aberystwyth, 1926.

FIRTH, SIR CHARLES. *Cromwell's Army.* London, 1912.

— 'Royalist and Cromwellian Armies in Flanders', *Transactions of the Royal Historical Society*, New Series, vol. XVII (1903), pp. 67–119.

GARDINER, S. R. *History of the Great Civil War, 1642–49.* London, 1893.

HAMPER, WILLIAM. *The Life, Diary and Correspondence of Sir William Dugdale.* 1872.

HINTON, MICHAEL. *A History of the town of Reading.* London, 1954.

LYTTON SELLS, A., *Memoirs of James II*, London, 1961.

PEACOCK, EDWARD. *Army Lists of the Roundheads and Cavaliers.* London, 1894.

PHILLIPS, J. ROLAND. *The Civil War in Wales and the Marches.* London, 1874.

UNDERDOWN, DAVID. *Royalist Conspiracy in England, 1649–60.* Yale, 1963.

WARBURTON, ELIOT. *Memoirs of Prince Rupert and the Cavaliers.* London, 1849.

WILKINSON, CLENNELL. *Prince Rupert, the Cavalier.* London, 1934.

Index

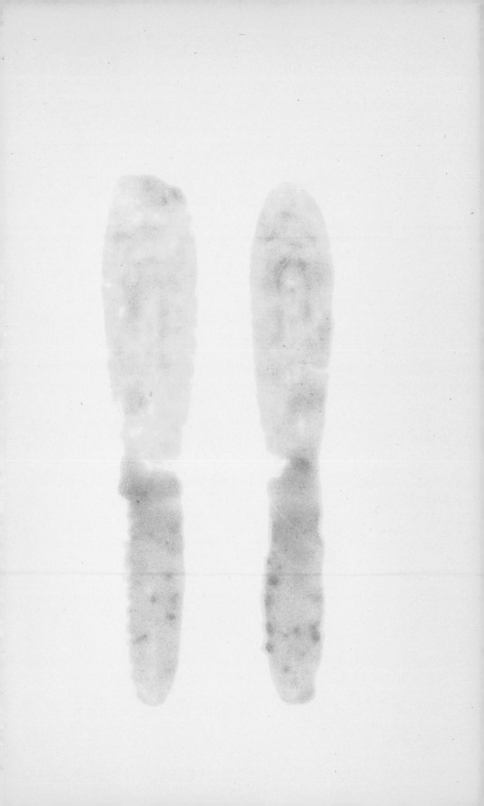

90510

THE CIVIL W